OXFORD SKILLS WORLD

Reading

WITH Writing

3

Yoko Mia Hirano

OXFORD
UNIVERSITY PRESS

OXFORD
UNIVERSITY PRESS

198 Madison Avenue
New York, NY 10016 USA

Great Clarendon Street, Oxford, OX2 6DP, United Kingdom

Oxford University Press is a department of the University of Oxford.
It furthers the University's objective of excellence in research, scholarship,
and education by publishing worldwide. Oxford is a registered trade
mark of Oxford University Press in the UK and in certain other countries

ISBN: 978 0 19 411350 2 Student Book with Workbook

Printed in China

This book is printed on paper from certified and well-managed sources

ACKNOWLEDGMENTS

Oxford University Press would like to thank all of the teachers whose opinions helped to
inform this series, and in particular, the following reviewers: Soo Ah Chung, Hwarang
Elementary School; Marta Juanet, Betania-patmos; Sedef Toksöz Kaykın,
Denizli Pamukkale Unv Egitim Vakfi okullari (PEV Koleji); Jeehee Moon,
T.T.R.; Jacob Rod, WILS Language School; Yuechun Wang, Phoenix City
International School

Cover illustration and main character illustrations by: Shane McGowan/The
Organisation

Back cover photograph: Oxford University Press building/David Fisher

Student Book

Illustrations by: Robin Boyer/Illustration Online pp.16, 40, 74, 82; Mattia Cerato/
MB Artists pp.26, 72; Monique Dong/Bright Group pp.27, 29; Lalena Fisher
pp.8, 18, 25, 30, 50, 51, 80, 81; Peter Francis/MB Artists pp.44, 83, 84, 85;
Angie Jones pp.13, 64; John Kurtz pp.11, 12, 22, 38, 39, 53, 78; Anthony Lewis/
MB Artists pp.15, 36, 42, 43, 54, 66, 71; Margeaux Lucas/MB Artists pp.37, 52,
70, 86; Julissa Mora pp.55, 57, 68, 88; Kim Soderburg/Illustration Online pp.65,
67; John White/The Neis Group p.23

The Publishers would like to thank the following for their kind permission to
reproduce photographs and other copyright material: 123rf: pp.9 (boy in smock/
Richard Semik), 13 (glue stick/Alexandr Makarov), 23 (puffy jacket/
Oleksii Demidov), (floppy hat/Watchara Kongton), (red shirt/Olga Popova),
28 (black shoes/satina), 37 (library books/dolgachov), (people in park/
Михаил Никитин), 51 (male lifeguard/Wavebreak Media Ltd), (actress/
Nicoleta Ifrim-Ionescu), 55 (female farmer/Kostic Dusan), (female salesclerk/
Dmitry Kalinovsky), 56 (artist painting/Iakov Filimonov), 60 (teacher with
children/dolgachov), 69 (car in garage/Danila Krylov), (room being swept/
dolgachov), 76–77 (children at cinema/Tyler Olson), 78 (watering plants/
bouvier sandrine), 83 (boy biking/Jacek Chabraszewski), (boy playing piano/
Aliaksei Lasevich), (girl with tablet/raywoo); Alamy: pp.34–35 (city satellite
photo/Aerial Archives), 69 (house in mountains/Traveller), 83 (girl reading
book/Hero Image Inc.); Getty: pp.cover (girl jumping over stream/Johner
Images; 20–21 (Inuit hunter/Ton Koene photography), 51 (photographer
on mountain/pixdeluxe); Oxford University Press: pp.9 (small water bottle/
Evikka/Shutterstock), 13 (horse in field/Anastasija Popova/Shutterstock),
27 (blue dress/Africa Studio/Shutterstock), (child's jumper/Nadezda Cruzova/
Shutterstock), 37 (bakery/Ariadna de Raadt/Shutterstock), 41 (train station/
Pagina/Shutterstock), (factory workers/Vasily Smirnov/Shutterstock), 55 (pilot
in cockpit/Andres Rodriguez/123rf), 65 (red couch/Fabian Schmidt/123rf),
(living room/Gorin/Shutterstock), (kitchen/Baloncici/Shutterstock), (table
lamp/Africa Studio/Shutterstock), 69 (bathroom/JPagetRFPhotos/Shutterstock);
Shutterstock: pp.6–7 (metal art/Su Justen), 8 (sculpture/Alex_Tu), 9 (girl
painting/ImagoPhoto), (yellow paint/Zurbagan), (paintbrush/Picsfive), (table/
donatas1205), (door/Elena Elisseeva), 10 (water bottles/AlenKadr), (table/

White Smoke), (door/MR.RAWIN TANPIN), (paint buckets/Africa Studio),
13 (open laptop/Vtls), (black magnet/Antonsov85), (ball of string/evalogan),
(blue tape dispenser/Stock Up), 14 (red tape dispenser/jeabsam), (ball of string/
Kitch Bain), (three magnets/Evgeny Starkin), (three glue sticks/N Azlin Sha),
19 (pencil, reused on pp.47, 61, 75, 89/almaje), 22 (blue backpack/Andrew
Buckin), (green backpack/Patricia Hofmeester), 23 (white feather/Konstanttin),
(red gloves/ratmaner), (green socks/Coprid), (hiking boots/al1962), (blue
jacket/Olga Kovalenko), (snow jacket/Karkas), (bobble hat/tam_odin), (long
sleeved shirt/Evikka), (snow boots/Christi Tolbert), 27 (pink skirt/indigolotos),
(blue jeans/Elnur), (brown shoes/Shane White), (child's trousers/windu),
28 (dress with sleeves/Ruslan Kudrin), (brown trousers/studio BM), (blue
jumper/Ruslan Kudrin), 32 (jumble sale/Jamie Hooper), 37 (office workers/
Dragon Images), (bus station/Axel Bueckert), (toy store/www.hollandfoto.net),
40 (stationery/WO Photography), 41 (reporter/2p.2play), (3D cinema audience/
Syda Productions), (gym/fiphoto), (shopping mall/Radu Bercan), (cobbler at
work/Toranico), 46 (map on phone/oatawa), 48–49 (firefighters/kaiskynet),
51 (female photographer/Tatiana Lysynchuk), (vet with dog/Nestor Rizhniak),
(baseball hitter/Tony-Gibson), (Female construction worker/Monkey Business
Images), 54 (female chef/xiuren), 55 (male potter/Odua Images), (female baker/
wavebreakmedia), (teacher and pupil/Monkey Business Images), 56 (female
pilot/TaraPatta), (chef with cake/sirtravelalot), (teacher with class/Monkey
Business Images), 58 (vet with cat/aspen rock), 62–63 (tree house/janken),
65 (child's bedroom/bezikus), (single bed/Ljupco Smokovski), 68 (red house/
almgren), 69 (hands being washed/Pikul Noorod), (dining room/Artazum),
69 (boys playing game/Frolphy), 79 (leaf fossil/halitomer), (girls studying
rock/wavebreakmedia), (boy swimming/Elena Nasledova), (children playing
catch/Nikodash), (boy shopping/Sergey Ryzhov), (girl reading/Michael C.
Gray), (girl with computer/goodluz), 83 (girl skateboarding/Elena Yakusheva),
(boys in tent/sirtravelalot)

Workbook

Illustrations by: John Kurtz pp.92, 99; Anthony Lewis/MB Artists p.113; Julissa
Mora pp.105, 107

The Publishers would like to thank the following for their kind permission to reproduce
photographs and other copyright material: 123rf: pp.92 (child in smock/Richard
Semik), 93 (glue stick/Alexandr Makarov), 95 (orange shirt/Olga Popova),
96 (floppy hat/Watchara Kongton), (orange shirt/Olga Popova), (child in
smock/Richard Semik), 100 (people in park/Михаил Никитин), (library books/
dolgachov), 101 (teacher with children/dolgachov), 104 (actress/Nicoleta
Ifrim-Ionescu), (male lifeguard/Wavebreak Media Ltd), 106 (female salesclerk/
Dmitry Kalinovsky), (female artist/Iakov Filimonov), (female farmer/Kostic
Dusan), 110 (room being swept/dolgachov), 112 (room being swept/dolgachov),
114 (boy biking/Jacek Chabraszewski), (boy playing piano/Aliaksei Lasevich),
(girl with tablet/raywoo); Oxford University Press: 91 (small water bottle/
Evikka/Shutterstock), 92 (small water bottle/Evikka/Shutterstock), 93 (horse
in field/Anastasija Popova/Shutterstock), 94 (horse in field/Anastasija Popova/
Shutterstock), 100 (bakery/Ariadna de Raadt/Shutterstock), 102 (train station/
Pagina/Shutterstock), 108 (living room/Gorin/Shutterstock), (kitchen/
Baloncici/Shutterstock), (table lamp/Africa Studio/Shutterstock), (red couch/
Fabian Schmidt/123rf); Shutterstock: 92 (table/donatas1205), (paint brush/
Picsfive), (yellow paint/Zurbagan), (green backpack/Patricia Hofmeester),
(door/Elena Elisseeva), 93 (blue tape dispenser/Stock Up), (magnet/
Antonsov85), 94 (open laptop/Vtls), (blue tape dispenser/Stock Up), (ball of
string/evalogan), 95 (child's trousers/windu), 96 (green socks/Coprid), (red
gloves/ratmaner), (hiking boots/al1962), (blue jacket/Olga Kovalenko), (blue
backpack/Andrew Buckin), 97 (snow boots/Christi Tolbert), 98 (pink skirt/
indigolotos), (brown shoes/Shane White), (blue jeans/Elnur), (brown trousers/
studio BM), 100 (bus station/Axel Bueckert), (office workers/Dragon Images),
(toy store/www.hollandfoto.net), (jumble sale/Jamie Hooper), 101 (shopping
mall/Radu Bercan), 102 (3D cinema audience/Syda Productions), (gym/fiphoto),
(shopping mall/Radu Bercan), 104 (vet with dog/Nestor Rizhniak), (female
photographer/Tatiana Lysynchuk), (female chef/xiuren), (baseball hitter/
Tony-Gibson), (female construction worker/Monkey Business Images), (female
reporter/2p.2play), 106 (female baker/wavebreakmedia), 108 (child's bedroom/
bezikus), (single bed/Ljupco Smokovski), (table/donatas1205), (office workers/
Dragon Images), 109 (red house/almgren), 110 (washing hands/Pikul Noorod),
(boys playing game/Frolphy), (dining room/Artazum), 111 (boy swimming/
Elena Nasledova), 112 (boys playing game/Frolphy), (girls studying rock/
wavebreakmedia), (girl with computer/goodluz), (boy shopping/Sergey
Ryzhov), (children playing catch/Nikodash), (baseball hitter/Tony-Gibson),
(girl reading/Michael C. Gray), 114 (girl skateboarding/Elena Yakusheva)

The manufacturer's authorised representative in the EU for product safety is Oxford University Press España S.A. of El Parque Empresarial San Fernando de Henares,
Avenida de Castilla, 2 – 28830 Madrid (www.oup.es/en or product.safety@oup.com).OUP España S.A. also acts as importer into Spain of products made by the manufacturer.

Table of Contents

Hi! I'm Olly.

TOPIC 1 — PAGE 6

Cool Projects

TOPIC 2 — PAGE 20

Clothes for Everyone!

Hi, I'm Molly!

TOPIC 3 — PAGE 34

Lost in the Big City!

TOPIC 4 — PAGE 48

What's Your Job?

TOPIC 5 — PAGE 62

Small Houses

TOPIC 6 — PAGE 76

Free Time

Introduction

Welcome to Oxford Skills World

Oxford Skills World: Reading with Writing is a flexible paired skills course that takes students on a journey toward independent learning, providing them with strategies and support to reach their goals.

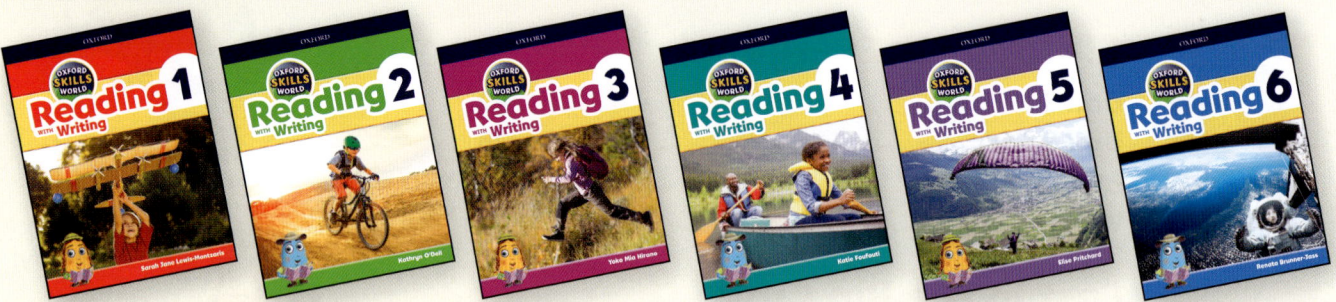

For Students

- Student Book / Workbook
- Student's website with downloadable audio and extra resources
  www.oup.com/elt/oxfordskillsworld

For Teachers

- Downloadable Teacher's Pack with instructional support, assessment, professional development videos, projects, and writing resources
- Classroom Presentation Tool
- Teacher's website with downloadable audio and extra resources
  www.oup.com/elt/teacher/oxfordskillsworld

Be the Leader on Your Skills Adventure!

Hi! We're Olly and Molly, your skills adventure guides. We help you reach your goals by introducing new reading and writing strategies, asking helpful questions, and giving friendly reminders. Most importantly, we cheer you on every step of the way! Let's go!

Quick Guide

Inside Each Topic

Topic Opener

Theme-based topics provide high-interest content relevant to students' lives.

My Goals introduces students to the objectives of each unit in the topic.*

Fun characters, Olly and Molly, encourage 21st century skills like critical thinking, collaboration, and communication.

Students answer questions to activate prior knowledge and think critically.

Get Ready to Read • Read

Reading Goals are strategies students can apply to any text.

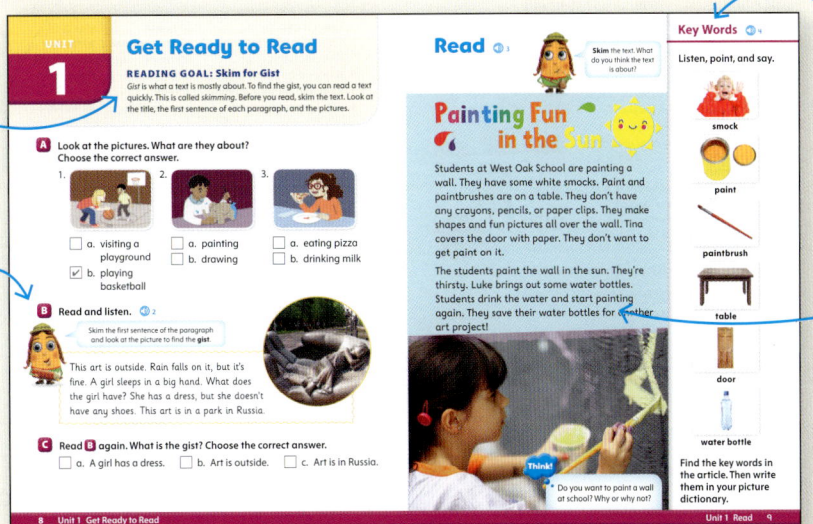

Olly and Molly guide students as they learn and apply new reading strategies.

Students learn new vocabulary for each text and complete the picture dictionary at the back of the book.

Students apply strategies to high-interest fiction and nonfiction texts, think critically about what they read, and make connections to their own lives.

*Each topic contains two thematically related units.

Quick Guide

Understand

Students increase their comprehension of the text by applying reading strategies to what they have read.

Students complete activities to strengthen their understanding of the unit's vocabulary.

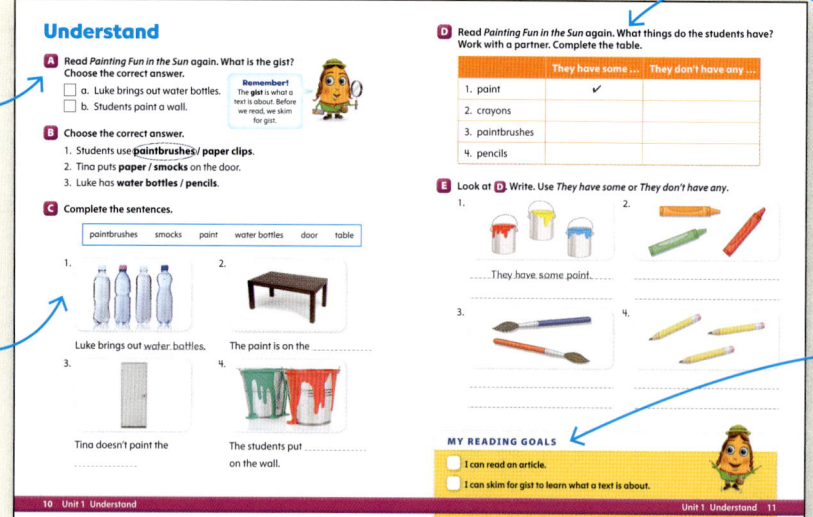

Students demonstrate comprehension of the unit's text, vocabulary, and grammar.

At the end of each unit, students assess the progress they have made toward achieving their goals.

Reading Check

With helpful reminders from Olly and Molly, students apply the **Reading Goals** from both units to a new text.

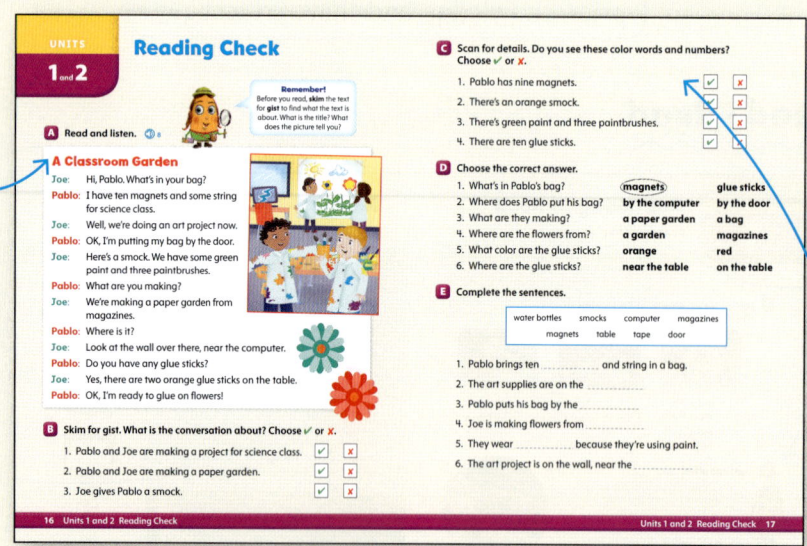

Students complete activities to boost comprehension and vocabulary application.

Get Ready to Write • Write

Writing Goals prepare students to write in different genres.

Writing Tips provide guidance on grammar, punctuation, and mechanics and help students write fluently and accurately.

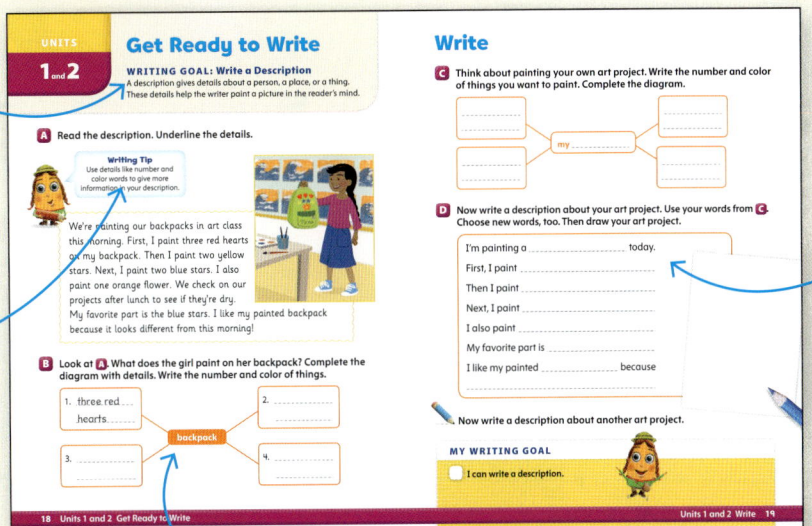

Scaffolded writing passages help students accomplish their writing goals.

Students use graphic organizers to comprehend model writing texts and to organize their thoughts for their own writing.

Workbook

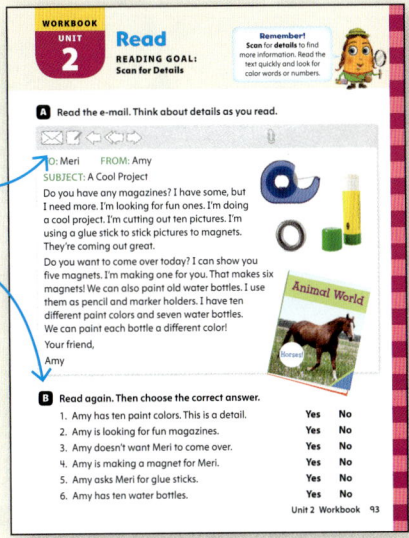

Workbook pages at the end of the book provide more opportunities for students to apply their **Reading Goals** and boost comprehension.

Additional activities provide extra opportunities for vocabulary comprehension and usage.

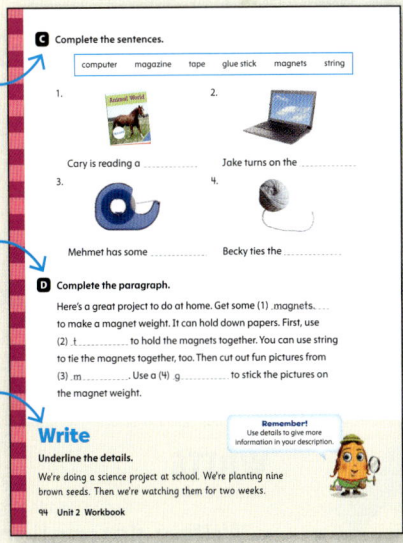

Students apply the topic's **Writing Tip** to ensure proper usage in their own writing.

Cool Projects

MY GOALS

UNIT 1

- Read the article *Painting Fun in the Sun*
- Skim for gist

UNIT 2

- Read the story *Milo Goes Fishing*
- Scan for details

WRITE

- Write a description

A Look at the picture. What do you see?

1. What are these things?
2. Do you want to make something from cans? Why or why not?

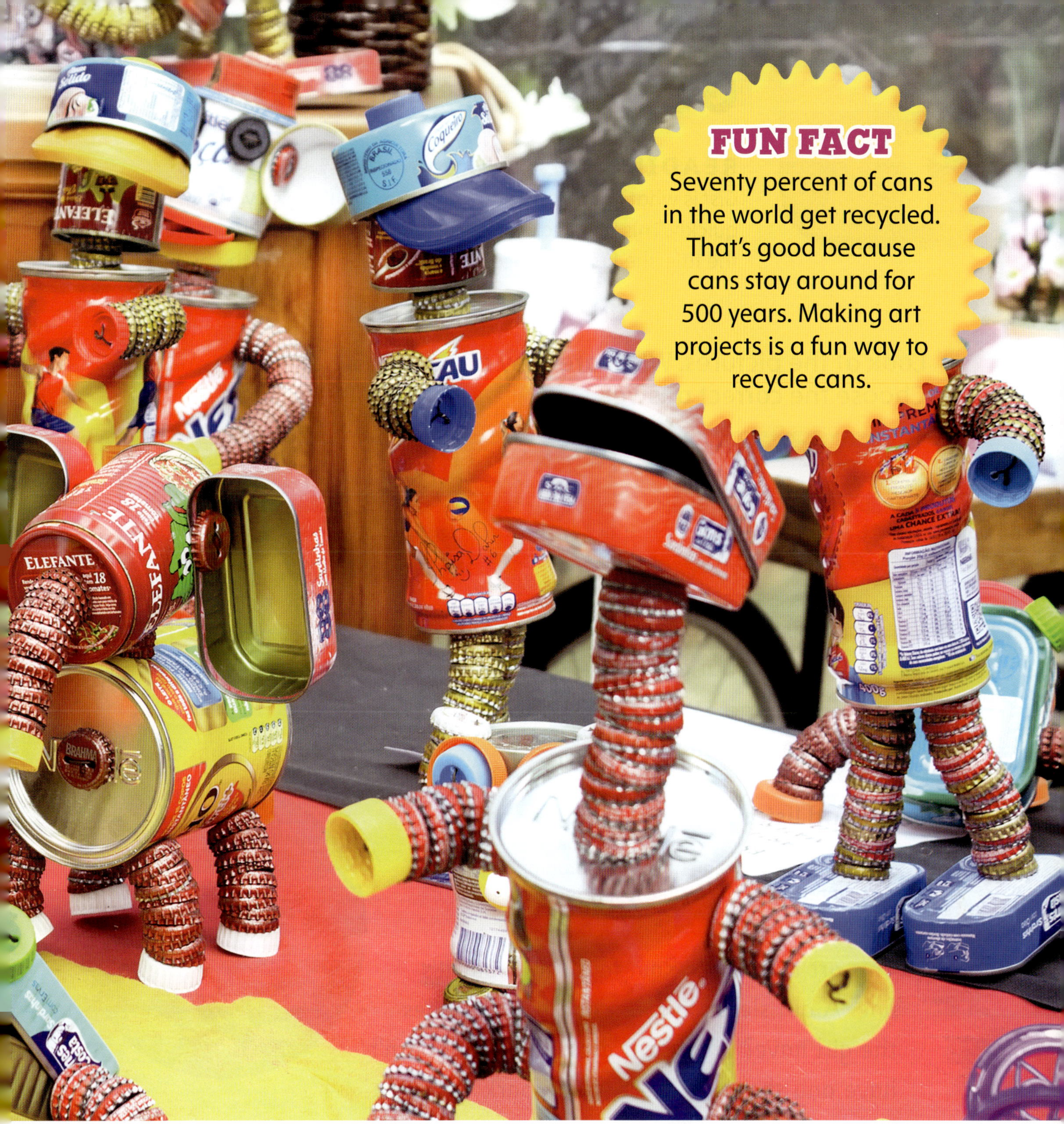

FUN FACT

Seventy percent of cans in the world get recycled. That's good because cans stay around for 500 years. Making art projects is a fun way to recycle cans.

B **Read the Fun Fact. Then answer the questions.**

1. How long do cans stay around?
2. Do you think this is a fun art project? Why or why not?

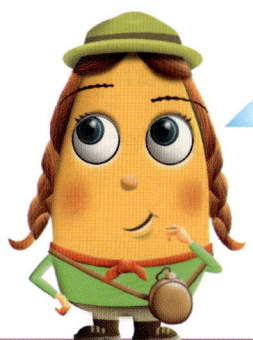

Think, Pair, Share
What art projects can you make?

Get Ready to Read

READING GOAL: Skim for Gist

Gist is what a text is mostly about. To find the gist, you can read a text quickly. This is called *skimming*. Before you read, skim the text. Look at the title, the first sentence of each paragraph, and the pictures.

A Look at the pictures. What are they about? Choose the correct answer.

1.

☐ a. visiting a playground
☑ b. playing basketball

2.

☐ a. painting
☐ b. drawing

3.

☐ a. eating pizza
☐ b. drinking milk

B Read and listen. 2

Skim the first sentence of the paragraph and look at the picture to find the **gist**.

This art is outside. Rain falls on it, but it's fine. A girl sleeps in a big hand. What does the girl have? She has a dress, but she doesn't have any shoes. This art is in a park in Russia.

C Read **B** again. What is the gist? Choose the correct answer.
☐ a. A girl has a dress.   ☐ b. Art is outside.   ☐ c. Art is in Russia.

Read 🔊 3

Skim the text. What do you think the text is about?

Painting Fun in the Sun

Students at West Oak School are painting a wall. They have some white smocks. Paint and paintbrushes are on a table. They don't have any crayons, pencils, or paper clips. They make shapes and fun pictures all over the wall. Tina covers the door with paper. They don't want to get paint on it.

The students paint the wall in the sun. They're thirsty. Luke brings out some water bottles. Students drink the water and start painting again. They save their water bottles for another art project!

Think!

Do you want to paint a wall at school? Why or why not?

Key Words 🔊 4

Listen, point, and say.

smock

paint

paintbrush

table

door

water bottle

Find the key words in the article. Then write them in your picture dictionary.

Understand

A Read *Painting Fun in the Sun* again. What is the gist? Choose the correct answer.

☐ a. Luke brings out water bottles.

☐ b. Students paint a wall.

> **Remember!**
> The **gist** is what a text is about. Before we read, we skim for gist.

B Choose the correct answer.

1. Students use **paintbrushes** / **paper clips**.

2. Tina puts **paper / smocks** on the door.

3. Luke has **water bottles / pencils**.

C Complete the sentences.

| paintbrushes | smocks | paint | ~~water bottles~~ | door | table |

1.

Luke brings out <u>water bottles.</u>

2.

The paint is on the _____

3.

Tina doesn't paint the _____

4.

The students put _____ on the wall.

D Read *Painting Fun in the Sun* again. What things do the students have? Work with a partner. Complete the table.

	They have some …	They don't have any …
1. paint	✔	
2. crayons		
3. paintbrushes		
4. pencils		

E Look at **D**. Write. Use *They have some* or *They don't have any*.

1.
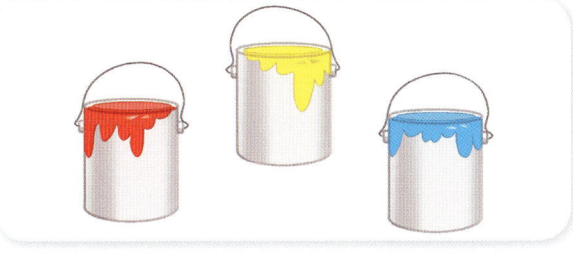
They have some paint.

2.
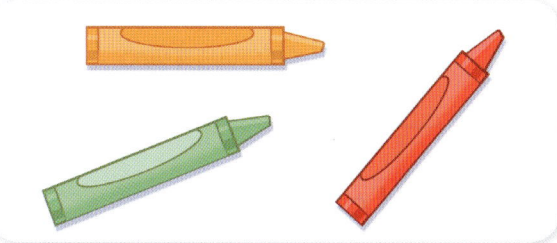

3.

4.

MY READING GOALS

☐ I can read an article.

☐ I can skim for gist to learn what a text is about.

Get Ready to Read

READING GOAL: Scan for Details

Details give more information about something in a text. To find details, quickly read the text a second time and look for only what you need, such as color words or numbers. This is called *scanning*.

A Look at the pictures. Choose the correct answer.

1.
A girl draws **two** / **four** trees.

2.
A boy has a **blue** / **green** marker.

3.
Sara uses **a red** / **one** paper clip.

B Read and listen. 5

These are **details**.

Sophie is happy at school today. She's working on an art project. Students paint ten cups. They cut green bottles. They tie white strings to the cups and bottles. The teacher hangs the art outside. It's pretty in the sun.

C Read **B** again. Are these details? Choose ✔ or ✘.

1. Sophie is making a project.

2. There are eight cups.

3. There is white string.

Read

After you read, **scan** for **details** like **colors** and **numbers**. What color are the magnets?

Milo Goes Fishing

Milo is bored with the games on his computer. His mom gives him black magnets, one ball of white string, three glue sticks, and some paper clips. "Do you have any magazines or tape?" asks Milo. "No," says his mom, "but you can make something fun."

Milo looks at the fish in the fishbowl and says, "I know! I can make a fishing game!" He ties one glue stick to string and makes a fishing pole. Then he ties one magnet to the end of his fishing pole string. He puts paper clips on the floor. Then he moves his pole to catch the paper clips. He's fishing!

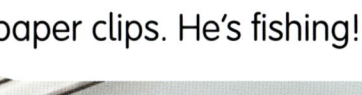

Think! Do you like Milo's game? Why or why not?

Key Words 7

Listen, point, and say.

computer

magnet

string

glue stick

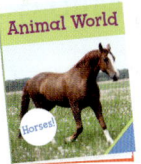

magazine

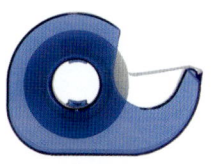

tape

Find the key words in the story. Then write them in your picture dictionary.

Understand

Remember!
Scan for **details** to look for the information you need quickly.

A Read *Milo Goes Fishing* again. Choose **Yes** or **No**.

1. There are black magnets.   (Yes)   No
2. There are two balls of string.   Yes   No
3. There is one glue stick.   Yes   No

B Choose the correct answer.

1. What does Milo have?
   ☐ a. magnets   ☐ b. tape
2. What does Milo ask for?
   ☐ a. games   ☐ b. magazines
3. What gives Milo an idea?
   ☐ a. the computer   ☐ b. the fish

C Complete the sentences with key words. Then match.

1. Milo gets black __magnets.__

2. Milo gets three _____

3. One of the materials is a ball of _____

4. Milo's mom doesn't have any magazines or _____

a.

b.

c.

1

d.

_____   _____   _____   _____

D Read *Milo Goes Fishing* again. What does Milo have? Complete the diagram. Work with a partner.

Does Milo have any … ? → **Yes, he does. / No, he doesn't.**

1. string → _____ Yes, he does. _____

2. magazines → _____

3. magnets → _____

4. tape → _____

E Look at **D**. Write. Use *Does Milo have any* in the questions. Use *Yes, he does* or *No, he doesn't* in the answers.

1.

   Does Milo have any string?

   Yes, he does.

2.

   _____

   _____

3.

   _____

   _____

4.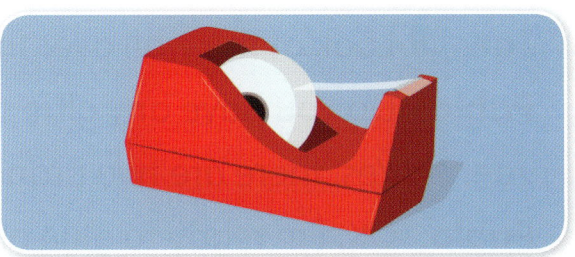

   _____

   _____

MY READING GOALS

☐ I can read a story.

☐ I can scan for details to find more information.

Reading Check

Remember!
Before you read, **skim** the text for **gist** to find what the text is about. What is the title? What does the picture tell you?

A **Read and listen.** 🔊 8

A Classroom Garden

Joe: Hi, Pablo. What's in your bag?

Pablo: I have ten magnets and some string for science class.

Joe: Well, we're doing an art project now.

Pablo: OK, I'm putting my bag by the door.

Joe: Here's a smock. We have some green paint and three paintbrushes.

Pablo: What are you making?

Joe: We're making a paper garden from magazines.

Pablo: Where is it?

Joe: Look at the wall over there, near the computer.

Pablo: Do you have any glue sticks?

Joe: Yes, there are two orange glue sticks on the table.

Pablo: OK, I'm ready to glue on flowers!

B **Skim for gist. What is the conversation about? Choose ✔ or ✘.**

1. Pablo and Joe are making a project for science class.

2. Pablo and Joe are making a paper garden.

3. Joe gives Pablo a smock.

C Scan for details. Do you see these color words and numbers? Choose ✔ or ✗.

1. Pablo has nine magnets.   ✔ ✗
2. There's an orange smock.   ✔ ✗
3. There's green paint and three paintbrushes.   ✔ ✗
4. There are ten glue sticks.   ✔ ✗

D Choose the correct answer.

1. What's in Pablo's bag?	(magnets)	glue sticks
2. Where does Pablo put his bag?	by the computer	by the door
3. What are they making?	a paper garden	a bag
4. Where are the flowers from?	a garden	magazines
5. What color are the glue sticks?	orange	red
6. Where are the glue sticks?	near the table	on the table

E Complete the sentences.

water bottles	smocks	computer	magazines
magnets	table	tape	door

1. Pablo brings ten _____ and string in a bag.

2. The art supplies are on the _____

3. Pablo puts his bag by the _____

4. Joe is making flowers from _____

5. They wear _____ because they're using paint.

6. The art project is on the wall, near the _____

Get Ready to Write

WRITING GOAL: Write a Description

A description gives details about a person, a place, or a thing. These details help the writer paint a picture in the reader's mind.

A Read the description. Underline the details.

> **Writing Tip**
> Use details like number and color words to give more information in your description.

We're painting our backpacks in art class this morning. First, I paint three red hearts on my backpack. Then I paint two yellow stars. Next, I paint two blue stars. I also paint one orange flower. We check on our projects after lunch to see if they're dry.
My favorite part is the blue stars. I like my painted backpack because it looks different from this morning!

B Look at **A**. What does the girl paint on her backpack? Complete the diagram with details. Write the number and color of things.

1. three red hearts

2. _____

backpack

3. _____

4. _____

Write

C Think about painting your own art project. Write the number and color of things you want to paint. Complete the diagram.

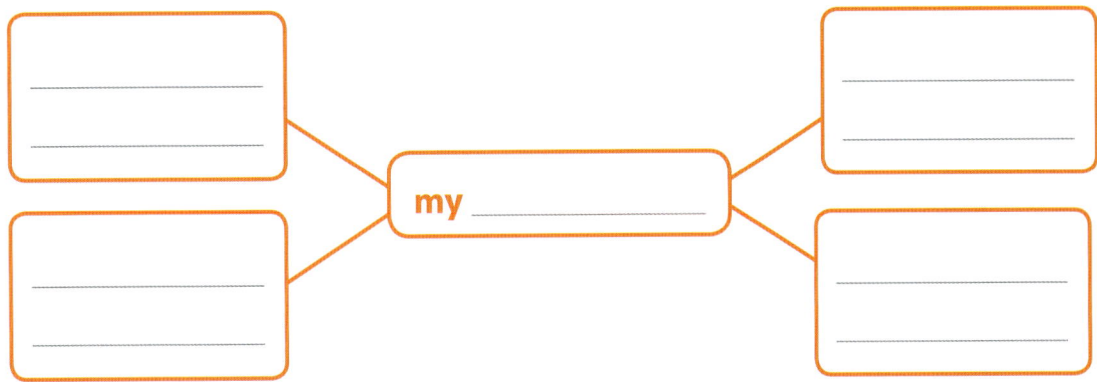

D Now write a description about your art project. Use your words from **C**. Choose new words, too. Then draw your art project.

I'm painting a _____ today.

First, I paint _____

Then I paint _____

Next, I paint _____

I also paint _____

My favorite part is _____

I like my painted _____ because

_____

Now write a description about another art project.

Clothes for Everyone!

MY GOALS

UNIT 3

- Read the article *Eddie Bauer's Big Idea*
- Find facts

UNIT 4

- Read the story *A Helping Hand*
- Find opinions

WRITE

- Write a persuasive text

A Look at the picture. What do you see?

1. What is the person doing?

2. Do you want to wear clothes like this?

FUN FACT

The Inuit live in the Arctic. It's a very cold part of the world. The Inuit make clothes from animals. These special clothes keep them warm outside.

B **Read the Fun Fact. Then answer the questions.**

1. Why do the Inuit wear special clothes?

2. Do you want to visit the Arctic? Why or why not?

Think, Pair, Share
What is your favorite piece of clothing?

Get Ready to Read

READING GOAL: Find Facts

A *fact* is something that is true for everyone. For example, *These socks are yellow* is a fact. When you read, find the facts to know what is true in a text.

A **Look at the pictures. Choose the facts.**

1.

☐ a. There are three pencils.

☐ b. The pencils are fun.

2.

☐ a. The book is pretty.

☐ b. The book has pink hearts.

3.

☐ a. Austin's backpack is blue.

☐ b. Austin's backpack is nice.

B **Read and listen.** 🔊 9

This is a **fact**.

The Super Backpack is $20.00. It's blue and holds two water bottles. The Top Backpack is $40.00. It's green and holds one water bottle. The Super Backpack is the best! Wear it and feel great! You save money, too.

$20.00

$40.00

C **Read B again. What is true? Choose the correct answer.**

☐ a. The Top Backpack is $20.00.

☐ b. The backpacks hold water bottles.

☐ c. The Super Backpack is the best.

Read 10

What is true information in this article? Underline one example.

Eddie Bauer's Big Idea

Eddie Bauer is on a fishing trip in the winter. He has special clothes to keep warm. He wears a soft hat on his head. He has warm gloves on his hands. On his feet are thick socks and boots. They keep his feet dry. He also wears a shirt under his jacket. Is this shirt heavy? Yes, it is. It's a heavy winter shirt.

Eddie thinks fishing in the winter is fun, but this time his jacket gets wet and he gets very cold. After he's home safe, he has an idea. He puts feathers inside jackets to make them puffy. Are these jackets warm? Yes, they are. People like the jackets, and Eddie sells lots of them.

Think!

Do you want a puffy jacket? Why or why not?

Key Words 11

Listen, point, and say.

hat

gloves

socks

boots

shirt

jacket

Find the key words in the article. Then write them in your picture dictionary.

Understand

A Read *Eddie Bauer's Big Idea* again. What is a fact? Choose the correct answer.

☐ a. Eddie Bauer goes on a fishing trip.

☐ b. Eddie Bauer doesn't think fishing is fun.

B Choose the correct answer.

1. Eddie's **jacket / hat** gets wet and he gets cold.

2. People wear **shirts / gloves** to keep their hands warm.

3. Eddie puts feathers in jackets to make them **heavy / puffy**.

C Complete the sentences.

| shirts | jackets | boots | socks | gloves | hats |

1.

Eddie sells lots of puffy

_____

2.

People wear _____

to keep their heads warm.

3.

It's very cold. People wear

a few more _____

4.

People wear _____

on their feet.

D Work with a partner. Complete the diagram.

Is this / Are these   Yes, it is. / Yes, they are.

1. _____Is this_____ hat soft?   →   _____Yes, it is._____

2. _____ gloves warm?   →   _____

3. _____ socks thick?   →   _____

4. _____ shirt heavy?   →   _____

E Look at **D**. Write. Use *Is this* for one thing. Use *Are these* for more than one thing.

1.

_____Is this hat soft? Yes, it is._____

2.

_____

3.

_____

4.

_____

MY READING GOALS

☐ I can read an article.

☐ I can find facts to know what is true in a text.

Get Ready to Read

READING GOAL: Find Opinions

An *opinion* is what a person thinks about something. It is not true for everyone. For example, *These socks are the best* is an opinion because it is not true for everyone. When you read, find opinions to know how people feel.

A Read. Which is an opinion? Choose the correct answer.

- [ ] a. I have a black shirt.
- [ ] b. This jacket is really nice.
- [ ] c. You wear gloves on your hands.

B Read and listen. 🔊 12

This is an **opinion**.

The Hat Family

My family likes hats. Today, Dad is wearing a purple hat. It's great. Mom is wearing an orange hat. It's pretty. My sister Meg is wearing a white hat. I'm wearing a green hat. It's the best one. We walk in the park and we're colorful!

C Read **B** again. Are these opinions? Choose ✔ or ✘.

1. My hat is the best. ☑✔ ☐✘
2. Mom is wearing an orange hat. ☐✔ ☑✘
3. Mom's hat is pretty. ☑✔ ☐✘
4. They walk in the park. ☐✔ ☑✘

Read 13

What **opinions** can you find in the story? Underline them.

A Helping Hand

Hee-Sun says, "Firefighters put out a fire at Isabella Diaz's house. Her family lost everything – their toys, books, and clothes. It's very sad." Hee-Sun's mom thinks for a minute. Then she leaves and comes back with clothes. She says, "Look. I like this green dress and these blue jeans and these black shoes. I like this skirt, too. I think it's pretty. I'm going to give these to Mrs. Diaz."

Hee-Sun runs to her bedroom and returns with her sister and her dad. Hee-Sun says, "They helped me pick these clothes for Isabella. They like this sweater. They think it's nice. And they like these long pants." Dad smiles and says, "And now I need help picking clothes for Mr. Diaz!"

Think!

Do you think Hee-Sun's mom has a good idea? Why or why not?

Key Words 14

Listen, point, and say.

dress

jeans

shoes

skirt

sweater

pants

Find the key words in the story. Then write them in your picture dictionary.

Understand

Remember!
An **opinion** is what a person thinks about something.

A Read *A Helping Hand* again.
Are these opinions? Choose **Yes** or **No**.

1. The Diaz family's house has a fire.   **Yes**   **No**
2. Hee-Sun's mom thinks a skirt is pretty.   **Yes**   **No**
3. Hee-Sun gets help choosing clothes.   **Yes**   **No**

B Choose the correct answer.

1. Why does Hee-Sun's mom want to help the Diaz family?
   ☐ a. She has lots of clothes.   ☐ b. The Diaz family needs clothes.
2. Who helps Hee-Sun choose clothes for Isabella?
   ☐ a. Hee-Sun's sister and dad   ☐ b. Mr. and Mrs. Diaz
3. What does Hee-Sun give her friend Isabella?
   ☐ a. a sweater and a dress   ☐ b. a sweater and pants

C Complete the sentences with key words. Then match.

1. Hee-Sun's dad and sister choose a nice _____
2. Hee-Sun's mom is giving a green _____
3. Hee-Sun has long _____ to give Isabella.
4. Hee-Sun's mom likes a pair of black _____

a.
_____

b.
_____

c.
_____

d.
_____

D Read *A Helping Hand* again. What does Hee-Sun's mom like? What do Hee-Sun's dad and sister like? Complete the table.

	She likes the …	They like the …
1. long pants		✔
2. pretty skirt		
3. nice sweater		
4. green dress		

E Look at **D**. Write. Use *She likes* or *They like*.

1.

They like the long pants.

2.

3.

4.

MY READING GOALS

☐ I can read a story.

☐ I can find opinions to know how people feel.

Reading Check

Remember!
Look for **facts** when you read.
What is true for everyone?
Look for **opinions**, too. What
isn't true for everyone?

A Read and listen. 15

Dear Grandma,

How are you? Is it hot in Florida? I'm inside a lot because it's really cold in Alaska and there's a lot of snow.

I think you are the best grandma! Thank you for sending me the sweater. I think it's nice. I like the color and the great buttons. I can wear it with pants or jeans. It feels super-warm.

On the next snowy day, I want to wear your sweater and my red jacket. I can wear two pairs of socks, boots, my winter hat, and gloves. Then I can go play in the snow with my friends!

Love,

Mark

B Look for the facts. What is true? Choose ✔ or ✗.

1. Mark is inside a lot.

2. Mark's grandma is the best grandma.

3. Mark sends Grandma a sweater.

C Look for the opinions. What does Mark think or feel? Choose ✔ or ✘.

1. The sweater is nice.   ☑✔ ☐✘

2. His grandma lives in Florida.   ☑✔ ☐✘

3. He wears a red jacket.   ☑✔ ☐✘

D Choose the correct answer.

1. Who gives Mark a sweater?
   ☐ a. Grandma
   ☐ b. Mom

2. It is very cold in _____
   ☐ a. Florida.
   ☐ b. Alaska.

3. Mark wears his sweater and a red _____ outside.
   ☐ a. jacket
   ☐ b. shirt

4. Where does Mark play with friends?
   ☐ a. inside
   ☐ b. in the snow

E Unscramble and match.

1. h i s t r
   _____shirt_____

2. l v o g e s
   _____

3. a t h
   _____

4. o o t b s
   _____

5. c j a t k e
   _____

6. k c o s s
   _____

a. This is for your head.

b. You wear this over a sweater.

c. You wear this under a sweater.

d. My hands wear these.

e. My feet wear these soft things.

f. You wear these to walk in snow.

Get Ready to Write

WRITING GOAL: Write a Persuasive Text

A persuasive text gives the writer's opinions about a topic. It also gives reasons why the writer thinks that way. Writers use persuasive texts because they want readers to agree with them.

A Read the e-mail. Underline *I think* and *I feel*.

Writing Tip
Use phrases like *I think* and *I feel* to write your opinions. Use *because* to give reasons.

To: All Students
From: Mr. Cho

We want to sell your old things to make money for a school trip.
I think clothes are nice because people like to wear them.
I feel toys are a good choice because children like to play with them.
I think books are great because people like to read them.
Please clean your closets and give us your old things.

B Look at **A**. What are good things to sell? What are the reasons? Complete the diagram.

Things		Reasons
1. _____clothes_____	→	_____People like to wear them._____
2. _____	→	_____
3. _____	→	_____

Write

C Think about good things to sell. Use your own words to give reasons. Complete the diagram.

Things   Reasons

1. _____ → _____

2. _____ → _____

3. _____ → _____

D Now write a persuasive text about something you want to make money for and things to sell. Use your words from **C**. Choose new words, too. Then draw the things you want to sell.

I want to _____

I think _____ because

_____

I feel _____ because

_____

I think _____ because

_____

Now write a persuasive text about another opinion you have.

MY WRITING GOAL

☐ I can write a persuasive text.

TOPIC

3

GEOGRAPHY

Lost in the Big City!

MY GOALS

UNIT 5

- Read the story *The Mystery of the Missing Ball*
- Find the problem and solution

UNIT 6

- Read the news story *Breaking News*
- Classify

WRITE

- Write a process paragraph

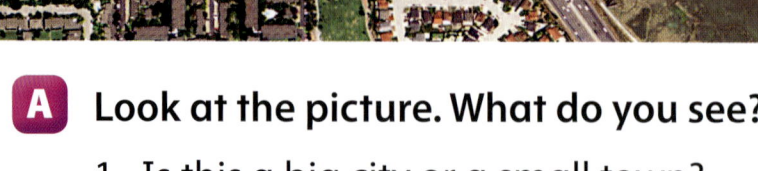 **Look at the picture. What do you see?**

1. Is this a big city or a small town?
2. What do you think the green parts are?

FUN FACT

Cameras high in the sky take photos of cities and towns around the world. You can see streets, buildings, and parks in the photos.

B Read the Fun Fact. Then answer the questions.

1. Where are the cameras that take these kind of photos?

2. Do you think these photos are helpful? Why or why not?

Think, Pair, Share
When do you use maps?

Get Ready to Read

READING GOAL: Find the Problem and Solution
Stories have problems and solutions. A *problem* is what goes wrong for a character. A *solution* is how the character fixes the problem. When you read, find the problem and solution to better understand the story.

A Omar is lost. How does he fix his problem? Order the pictures.

B Read and listen. 🔊 16

This is the **problem**. What is the **solution**?

Helping Grandma

My grandma loves to read, but her house is far from the bookstore. She can't get books. Where's the bookstore? It's next to my house. I can help Grandma because I can get books for her!

C Read **B** again. How does the girl help her grandmother? Choose the correct answer.

- [ ] a. She gets books from the bookstore.
- [ ] b. She reads to her grandmother.
- [ ] c. She goes to see her grandmother.

Read 17

What is wrong in the story? How can it be fixed?

The Mystery of the Missing Ball

Gordon pets his dog, Buddy, and says, "Mom, are you working at the office today? I need help finding my yellow ball." "No, I'm not working at the office," says Mom, "But I *am* going to the library to get books, and the bakery to buy cookies. Then I'm going to the bus station to pick up Grandma." Gordon asks, "Can Grandma and I go to the park and the toy store to look for my ball?" "Sure. Buddy needs a walk, so bring him with you." Gordon nods. Then he sits and asks his dog, "Buddy, do *you* know where my ball is?" Buddy runs off. Gordon follows him. There's the yellow ball in Buddy's bed!

Think!

How do you find lost things?

Key Words 🔊 18

Listen, point, and say.

office

library

bakery

bus station

park

store

Find the key words in the story. Then write them in your picture dictionary.

Understand

Remember!
A **problem** is what goes wrong. A **solution** is how the problem is fixed.

A Read *The Mystery of the Missing Ball* again. What is the problem and solution? Choose the correct answer.

☐ a. The dog is missing and Gordon finds him.

☐ b. The ball is missing and Buddy finds it.

B Choose the correct answer.

1. Gordon's mom is going to the **library / park**.

2. Gordon wants to look for the ball in **one place / two places**.

3. Mom says that **Buddy / Grandma** is coming over.

C Complete the sentences.

bakery	park	bus station	store	library	office

1.

Mom isn't working at the

_____

2.

Gordon wants to look for the

ball at the toy _____

3.

Gordon says he can bring

Buddy to the _____

4.

Mom is going to get books

from the _____

D Read *The Mystery of the Missing Ball* again. Where is Mom going? Where are Gordon and Grandma going? Work with a partner. Complete the diagram.

1. _library_

2. _____

She's going …

3. _____

4. _____

They're going …

5. _____

E Look at **D**. Write. Use *She's going* or *They're going*.

1.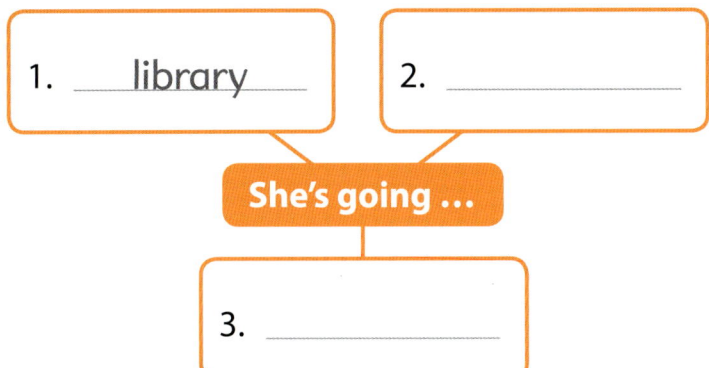

She's going to the bakery.

2.

_____

3.

_____

4.

_____

MY READING GOALS

☐ I can read a story.

☐ I can find the problem and solution to better understand the story.

Get Ready to Read

READING GOAL: Classify

To *classify* means to put things into a group because they are similar in some way. When you read, classify people, places, and things to understand what they have in common.

A Look at the picture. Where do you do things outside? Circle them. Where do you do things inside? Put an X over them.

B Read and listen. 🔊 19

We can **classify** things. These are big things.

Peter needs things for school. He goes to the store and buys paper clips, pencil sharpeners, and pencils. He needs a backpack and a big clock, but the store doesn't have them. The store sells only small things.

C Read **B** again. What small things does Peter need? Choose ✔ or ✘.

1. paper clips, pencils, pencil sharpeners

2. backpack, clock

3. backpack, pencils, clock

Read 🔊 20

How can you **classify** the animals?

Breaking News

Wendy Lee: Hello, I'm Wendy Lee. Animals are running around our city! I'm in the movie theater next to the bookstore. No one is watching the movie, because there's an elephant, a lion, and a bear here. They're big! On Elm Street, small monkeys and pandas are in the gym across from the train station. People are taking the train home because they can't exercise! Let's go to Rob West. He's at the shopping mall next to the old factory.

Rob West: Hi, Wendy. I'm in the shoe repair shop in the shopping mall. Everything is quiet here. I guess animals don't like to shop or have shoes fixed! Back to you, Wendy.

Think!
- Do you watch the news on TV? Why or why not?

Key Words 🔊 21

Listen, point, and say.

movie theater

gym

train station

shopping mall

factory

shoe repair shop

Find the key words in the news story. Then write them in your picture dictionary.

Understand

Remember!
Classify and put things into a group because they are similar in some way.

A Read *Breaking News* again.
Are the animals big or small? Choose **Yes** or **No**.

1. The elephant, lion, and bear are big.   **Yes**   **No**

2. The monkeys and pandas are small.   **Yes**   **No**

3. The monkeys and bear are small.   **Yes**   **No**

B Choose the correct answer.

1. Where are the big animals?

   ☐ a. at the train station   ☐ b. at the movie theater

2. What place do the small animals not go into?

   ☐ a. the factory   ☐ b. the gym

3. Where is it quiet?

   ☐ a. in the factory   ☐ b. in the shoe repair shop

C Complete the sentences with key words. Then match.

1. The small animals go to the _____ across from the train station.

2. The bear is at the _____

3. Rob West is in the _____ in the shopping mall.

4. The _____ is next to the factory.

a.

b.

c.

d.

_____   _____   _____   _____

D Read *Breaking News* again. Where are the places in Newton?
Work with a partner. Complete the table.

	Where	Other Place
1. shopping mall	next to	factory
2. gym		train station
3. shoe repair shop		shopping mall
4. movie theater		bookstore

E Look at **D**. Write.

1.

The shopping mall is next to the

factory.

2.

The gym is _____

_____

3.

The shoe repair shop is _____

_____

4.

The movie theater is _____

_____

MY READING GOALS

☐ I can read a news story.

☐ I can classify and understand how things are similar in some way.

Reading Check

Remember!
Look for the **problem** when you read. What is the **solution**? **Classify** when you read. What things are similar?

A Read and listen. 22

Bringing the Outside In!

I visit Helen in New York, but her mom has to work in her office and can't take us anywhere. I say, "It's OK. We can play inside." Helen says, "But that's boring, Abby. I want to go to the gym. And I want to see the flowers in the park."

I say, "Let's play that rooms are places. Your bedroom has books. It's the bookstore." Helen says, "Oh, I see. My living room has a TV. It's a movie theater."

I nod and say, "Your kitchen has cookies. It's the bakery!" Helen smiles and says, "Let's walk to the bakery for cookies." I say, "Sure. That's fun!"

B What is the problem and solution? Choose ✔ or ✘.

1. The girls can't go anywhere outside. They play that rooms are places.

2. The girls can't go to the bakery. They go to the movie theater.

3. The girls can't go anywhere outside. They watch TV.

C Look at the story. What can you classify as stores? Choose ✔ or ✘.

1. bookstore, gym   ✔ ✘
2. bakery, park   ✔ ✘
3. bakery, bookstore   ✔ ✘

D Choose the correct answer.

1. Who visits New York?	**Helen**	**Abby**
2. Why is Helen's mom busy?	**She's shopping.**	**She's working.**
3. Where does Helen want to go?	**the movie theater**	**the gym**
4. Where does Helen want to see flowers?	**the park**	**her bedroom**
5. What is Helen's room?	**the bookstore**	**the office**
6. What is the kitchen?	**the gym**	**the bakery**

E Complete the sentences.

> bakery   office   shopping mall   gym   library
>
> movie theater   park   bookstore

1. Helen wants to see the flowers in the _____

2. Helen also wants to go to the _____

3. Helen's bedroom has a lot of books. Abby says it's a _____

4. The living room has a TV. Helen says it's a _____

5. Helen's kitchen is a _____

6. Helen's mom is busy with work in her _____

Get Ready to Write

WRITING GOAL: Write a Process Paragraph

A process paragraph explains how to do something. It can include steps or give directions.

A Read the paragraph. Underline the sequence words.

> **Writing Tip**
> Use sequence words such as *first*, *then*, *next*, and *finally* to show the order of things in a process.

A GPS Can Help

A GPS is a special tool that tells you how to get to places. Are you going to the bakery, the park, or the movie theater? The GPS can tell you the way. First, decide where you want to go. For example, you want to go to a store. Then put the address into the GPS. Next, the GPS shows you the directions on a map. Finally, follow the directions and you are on your way!

B Look at **A**. What is the process? Complete the diagram.

First,

1. <u>decide where to go.</u>

Then

2. _____

Next,

3. _____

Finally,

4. _____

Write

C Think about using another special tool. What are the steps? Complete the diagram.

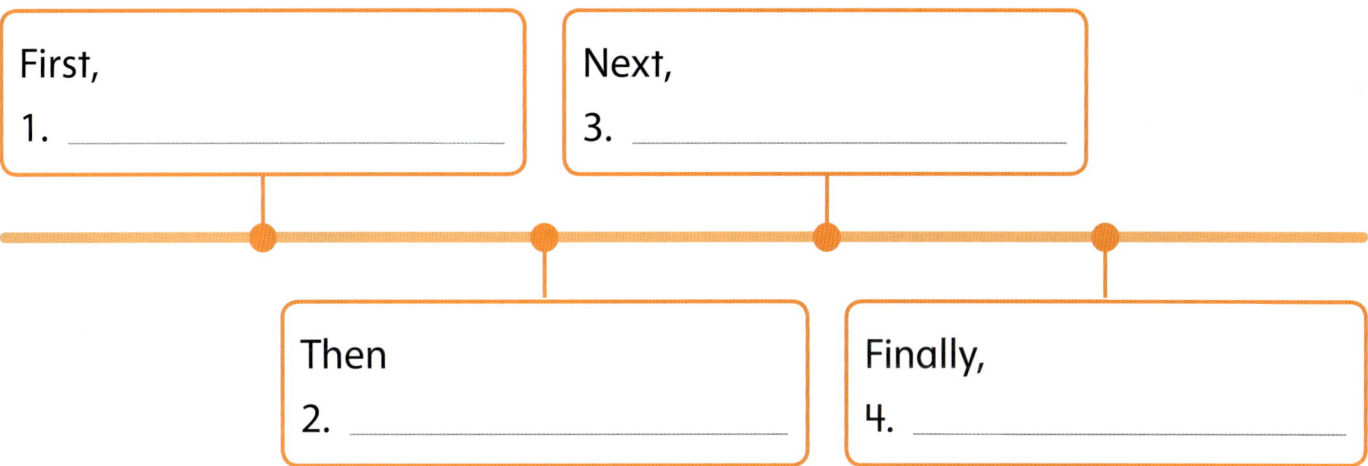

First,
1. _____

Next,
3. _____

Then
2. _____

Finally,
4. _____

D Now write a process paragraph about your special tool. Use your words from **C**. Choose new words, too. Then draw a picture of the tool.

A _____ can _____

First, _____

Then _____

Next, _____

Finally, _____

Now write a process paragraph about another special tool.

MY WRITING GOAL

☐ I can write a process paragraph.

TOPIC

4

CITIZENSHIP

What's Your Job?

MY GOALS

UNIT 7

- Read the article *Dangerous Jobs*
- Make notes

UNIT 8

- Read the story *Who Put the Fire Out?*
- Summarize

WRITE

- Write an outline

A **Look at the picture. What do you see?**

1. What are these people doing?

2. What do you need to know to do this job?

FUN FACT

Firefighters wear special clothes to fight fires. The clothes keep them safe from fire and heat. Some of these clothes weigh 45 kilograms.

B **Read the Fun Fact. Then answer the questions.**

1. How much do the clothes firefighters wear weigh?

2. Do you think firefighters like their job? Why or why not?

Think, Pair, Share
What job do you want to have?

Get Ready to Read

READING GOAL: Make Notes

Notes are words or phrases you write down as you read. Use notes to help you remember and think about important information in a text.

A Look at the pictures. What are notes? Choose ✔ or ✘.

1.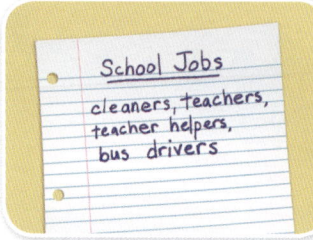
2.
3.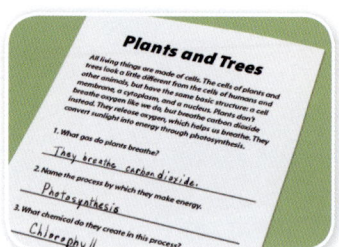

B Read and listen. 🔊 23

Notes are important information you write down as you read.

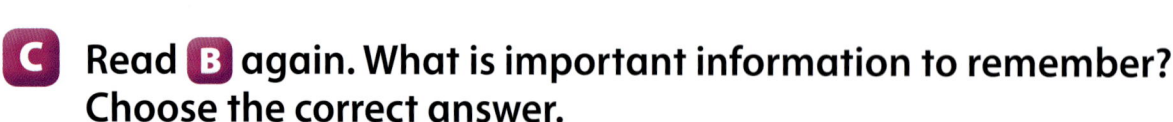

Soccer Players

Lots of people want to be a soccer player. It's a very popular sport around the world. Many soccer players start playing when they are only three or four years old. They work hard and have good teamwork!

soccer = popular
work + teamwork

C Read **B** again. What is important information to remember? Choose the correct answer.

☐ a. Soccer is a popular sport.

☐ b. Soccer players are popular.

☐ c. Soccer players are on good teams.

Read 🔊 24

*What words are good **notes** for actors, baseball players, and builders? Underline them.*

Dangerous Jobs

Think about jobs around the world. Which ones aren't safe? Lifeguards save people from water at beaches or pools. Photographers can take photos in storms or high places. Veterinarians can care for tigers or lions. Actors can act in car chases and get hurt. Baseball players aren't always safe. A fast ball can break their bones or hurt them. Builders are safe most of the time, but they can hurt their fingers with tools. Some jobs are safer than others, but there is a little danger in any job.

> Job   Danger
> lifeguards → water at pools + beaches
> photographers → storms + high places
> veterinarians → lions + tigers

Think!

What other jobs do you think are dangerous?

Key Words 🔊 25

Listen, point, and say.

lifeguard

photographer

veterinarian

actor

baseball player

builder

Find the key words in the article. Then write them in your picture dictionary.

Understand

Remember!
Write down important information as you read.

A Read *Dangerous Jobs* again. Which note is helpful to remember? Choose the correct answer.

☐ a. photographers ➜ photos

☐ b. baseball players ➜ hurt by a fast ball

B Choose the correct answer.

1. A **veterinarian / lifeguard** can take care of a tiger.

2. A **builder / photographer** can work outside in a storm.

3. A ball can hit **actors / baseball players** in a game.

C Complete the sentences.

| builder | actors | photographer | baseball player | lifeguards | veterinarian |

1.

A _____ uses tools.

2.

_____ save people from water.

3.

A _____ can care for scary animals.

4.

A _____ can take pictures in dangerous places.

D Read *Dangerous Jobs* again. What can be dangerous for the people with these jobs? Complete the diagram. Work with a partner.

Job	Dangerous Part of Job
1. photographers →	can take photos in storms
2. baseball players →	_____
3. actors →	_____
4. builders →	_____

E Look at **D**. Write. Use *can* to write about each job.

1.

   Photographers can take photos in storms.

2.

   _____
   _____

3.

   _____
   _____

4.

   _____
   _____

MY READING GOALS

☐ I can read an article.

☐ I can make notes to help me remember important information.

Get Ready to Read

READING GOAL: Summarize

Summarize means to tell what a story is about in one or two sentences. To summarize a story, retell the story in your own words after you read.

A **Look at the picture. What do you see? Summarize.**

B **Read and listen.** 26

Summarizing is telling what the story is about in one or two sentences.

My mom didn't have a job for a while. She was a cook at Seoul Kitchen, but it closed. Today, she went to a new restaurant. She asked for a job, and she got it. We aren't surprised. She's a great cook!

C **Read B again. Which sentence best summarizes the story? Choose ✔ or ✘.**

1. Mom is a cook.

2. Seoul Kitchen closed.

3. Mom gets a new job.

Read 🔊 27

After you read, **summarize** the story in your own words.

Who Put the Fire Out?

An artist is painting a cake on the bakery window. A farmer stops and says, "That's a nice cake! I work on a farm. Do you paint farms?" The artist can't answer, because there's a fire in the bakery!

The baker doesn't know what to do. The salesclerk says, "I sell things. I don't put out fires." A teacher is getting bread. He says, "I teach students. I can't put out a fire." A pilot is getting a cake, and she says, "I'm a pilot! I fly planes. Sometimes there's a fire on the plane." She puts out the fire. Everybody claps!

Think!

What other jobs might have to put out fires? Why?

Listen, point, and say.

artist

farmer

baker

salesclerk

teacher

pilot

Find the key words in the story. Then write them in your picture dictionary.

Understand

A Read *Who Put the Fire Out?* again. Does the sentence summarize the text? Choose **Yes** or **No**.

1. The artist paints the bakery window. **Yes** **No**

2. The baker doesn't know what to do. **Yes** **No**

3. There's a fire in the bakery and a
   pilot puts it out. **Yes** **No**

B Choose the correct answer.

1. What stops the artist from answering the farmer?
   ☐ a. the farmer talking   ☐ b. the fire in the bakery

2. What does the salesclerk say?
   ☐ a. He doesn't put out fires.   ☐ b. He teaches students.

3. What is the pilot getting?
   ☐ a. bread   ☐ b. a cake

C Complete the sentences with key words. Then match.

1. The _____ is painting a cake.

2. The _____ doesn't know what to do.

3. The _____ works with students.

4. Everybody claps for the _____

a.    b.    c.    d.

_____   _____   _____   _____

D Read *Who Put the Fire Out?* again. What do they do? Complete the table. Work with a partner.

	What do they do?
1. a salesclerk	sell things
2. a pilot	
3. a teacher	
4. a farmer	

E Look at **D**. Write. Use the correct form of the verb phrase.

1.

A salesclerk sells things.

2.

3.

4.

MY READING GOALS

☐ I can read a story.

☐ I can summarize and tell what a story is about in one or two sentences.

Reading Check

A Read and listen. 🔊 29

Interview with a Veterinarian

Peter: Thank you for this interview, Dr. Das.

Dr. Das: Of course, Peter.

Peter: First, what do veterinarians do?

Dr. Das: They take care of animals.

Peter: Do you like the job?

Dr. Das: Yes, I love animals.

Peter: Did you always want to be a vet?

Dr. Das: No. I wanted to be an actor or a baker.

Peter: Really? Why did you change your mind?

Dr. Das: A nice farmer had a sick horse that I wanted to help.

Peter: My grandpa has a farm.

Dr. Das: That nice farmer was your grandfather.

Peter: Wow, I didn't know that!

B Which notes are for this text? Choose ✔ or ✘.

1. Dr. Das takes care of animals.

2. Peter likes animals.   ✘

3. Dr. Das has a farm.

C What is a summary of the interview? Choose ✔ or ✘.

1. Dr. Das wanted another job, but changed his mind. ✔ ✘

2. Dr. Das takes care of animals. ✔ ✘

3. Dr. Das knows Peter's grandfather. ✔ ✘

D Choose the correct answer.

1. As a child, Dr. Park wanted to be an actor or a _____
   - ☐ a. baker.
   - ☐ b. pilot.

2. Peter's grandfather has a _____
   - ☐ a. farm.
   - ☐ b. bakery.

3. Dr. Park wanted to be a veterinarian because he _____
   - ☐ a. liked the farm.
   - ☐ b. wanted to help a sick horse.

E Unscramble and match.

1. a r e r f m
   _____ •   • a. The _____ paints flowers.

2. c k l e r s l a e s
   _____ •   • b. The _____ wears a hard hat.

3. d r e l i b u
   _____ •   • c. The _____ works in the fields.

4. e b r a k
   _____ •   • d. The _____ works in the store.

5. h p t o o r g a h p r e •   • e. The _____ likes taking pictures.

6. t t i s a r
   _____ •   • f. The _____ is making bread.

Get Ready to Write

WRITING GOAL: Write an Outline

An *outline* is a plan for your writing. It is a list that helps you organize your thoughts. An outline shows the order of the ideas you want to write about.

A Read the paragraph about jobs.

> **Writing Tip**
> Use numbers to show the main ideas in your outline. Use bullet points to show the details.

Today in class, the students are talking about jobs. They think Max wants to be a baker. Max says he doesn't want to be a baker because he doesn't like bread or cookies. Also, he doesn't like standing on his feet all day. Max does want to be a pilot because he likes to go places around the world. Also, he likes planes!

B Look at **A**. What is the order of the ideas in the paragraph? Complete the outline for Max.

1. Max doesn't want to be a _____baker._____

   • doesn't like _____

   • doesn't like _____

2. Max wants to be a _____

   • likes _____

   • likes _____

Write

C Think about jobs. What don't you want to be? What do you want to be? Complete the outline.

1. I don't want to be a _____
   - I don't like _____
   - I don't like _____
2. I want to be a _____
   - I like _____
   - I like _____

D Now write a paragraph about jobs. Use your words from **C**. Choose new words, too. Then draw the job you want.

I don't want to be a _____

_____

_____

I want to be a _____

_____

_____

Now write about a friend. What doesn't he or she want to be? What does he or she want to be? Why?

MY WRITING GOAL

☐ I can write an outline.

Small Houses

MY GOALS

UNIT 9

- Read the story *The Case of the Missing Glasses*
- Identify the main and minor characters

UNIT 10

- Read the article *Small Houses, Big Heart*
- Understand the setting

WRITE

- Write a journal entry

 **Look at the picture. What do you see?**

1. Where is this small house?
2. What do you think is inside the house?

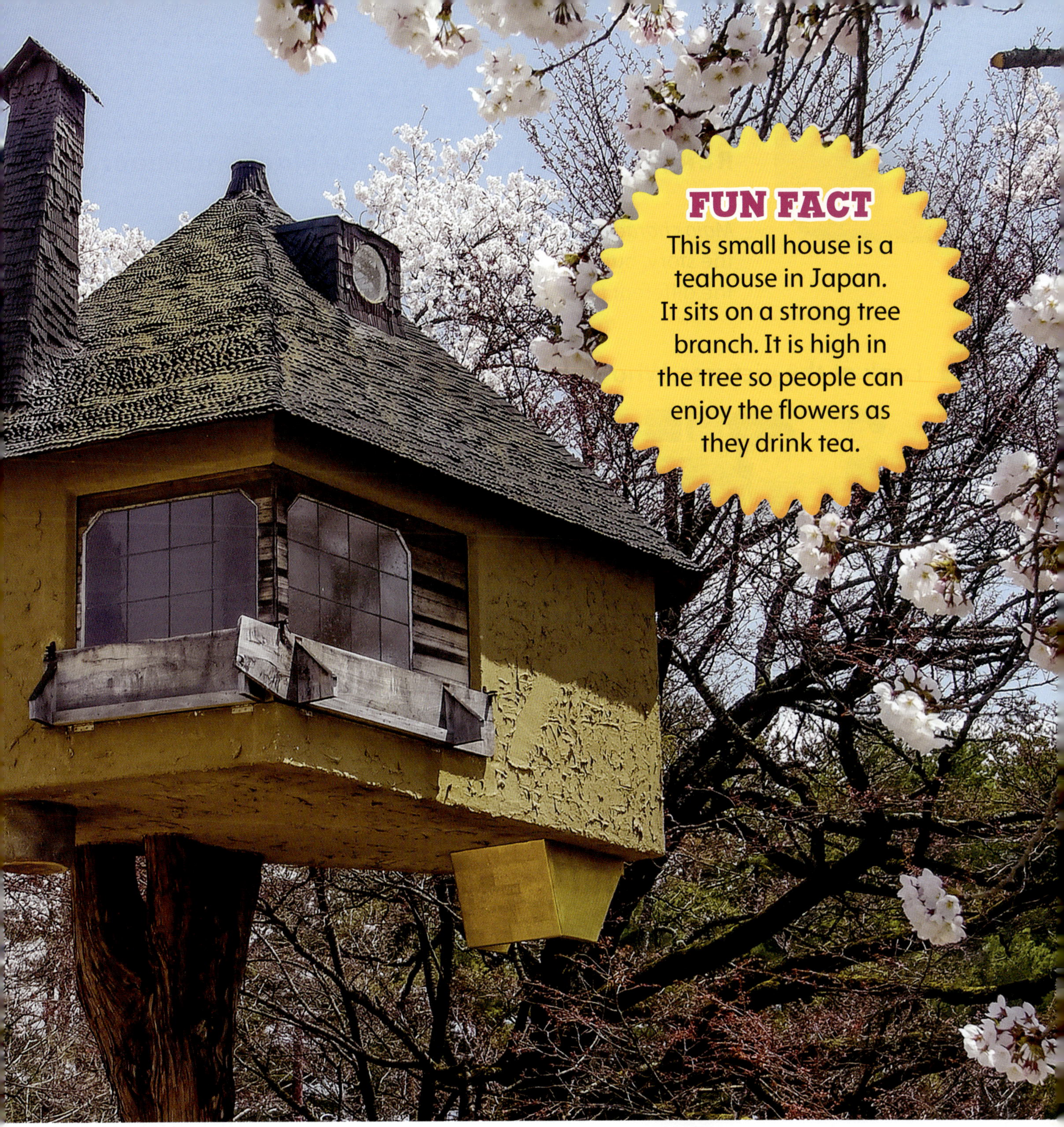

FUN FACT

This small house is a teahouse in Japan. It sits on a strong tree branch. It is high in the tree so people can enjoy the flowers as they drink tea.

B **Read the Fun Fact. Then answer the questions.**

1. What can you drink in this small house?
2. Do you like this house? Why or why not?

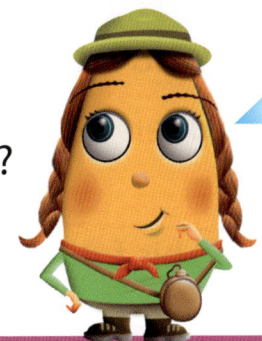

Think, Pair, Share
What is good about small houses?

Get Ready to Read

READING GOAL: Identify the Main and Minor Characters

Main characters are who the story is about. *Minor characters* are in the story, but the story isn't about them. When you read, identify the different types of characters in a story.

A Look at the pictures. Who is the main character? Circle.

B Read and listen. 🔊 30

This is the **main character**.

The Birdhouse Builder

Julian builds a birdhouse. He uses small tree branches, glue, string, and paint. Julian's dad helps Julian put the birdhouse on a big tree near their house. Now the birds have a small, cozy place to live.

C Read **B** again. Who is the minor character? Choose the correct answer.

- [ ] a. Julian's father
- [ ] b. Julian
- [ ] c. Julian and his father

Read 🔊 31

Who is the **main character** in the story? Underline the name.

The Case of the
Missing Glasses

Saturday was a very bad day for Ahmet. He lost his glasses, and he needed them right away. He wanted to read a book about his favorite superhero.

Where were his glasses? Were they on the couch in the living room? Ahmet looked. No, they weren't. Were they in the kitchen, next to the red lamp? His mom looked. No, they weren't. Were they in his bedroom, under his bed? His little brother looked. No, they weren't.

Then Ahmet remembered! He ran outside to his playhouse made of tree branches, rocks, and an old towel. He quickly went inside, and there were his glasses … right next to the book about his favorite superhero!

Think!

Do you often lose things? What things do you lose?

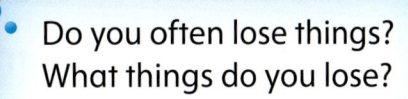

Key Words 🔊 32

Listen, point, and say.

couch

living room

kitchen

lamp

bedroom

bed

Find the key words in the story. Then write them in your picture dictionary.

Understand

A Read *The Case of the Missing Glasses* again. Who are the minor characters? Choose the correct answer.

☐ a. Ahmet and his mom

☐ b. Ahmet's mom and his little brother

Remember!
Identify the **main characters** to know who the story is about.

B Choose the correct answer.

1. Ahmet's **bed / playhouse** is made of tree branches and rocks.

2. Ahmet's little brother looked in the **bedroom / kitchen**.

3. The playhouse is **inside / outside** Ahmet's house.

C Complete the sentences.

kitchen	bedroom	couch	lamp	bed	living room

1.

Ahmet's glasses weren't under his _____

2.

Ahmet's mom looked for the glasses in the _____

3.

The _____ in the kitchen is red.

4.

There is a _____ in Ahmet's living room.

D Read *The Case of the Missing Glasses* again. Where were Ahmet's glasses? Complete the diagram. Work with a partner.

Were they in … ? **Yes, they were. / No, they weren't.**

1. the living room	→	No, they weren't.
2. the kitchen	→	
3. the bedroom	→	
4. the playhouse	→	

E Look at **D**. Write. Use *Were* in the question. Use *Yes, they were* or *No, they weren't* in the answer.

1.

Were they in the living room?

No, they weren't.

2.

3.

4.

MY READING GOALS

☐ I can read a story. ☐ I can identify the main and minor characters to know who the story is about.

Get Ready to Read

READING GOAL: Understand the Setting

The *setting* is the time and place of a text. It answers the questions *When?* and *Where?* When you read, identify the setting and ask *How does this setting affect the people in the text?*

A Look at the pictures. Choose the setting for each one.

1.

☐ a. a farm at night
☐ b. a bakery in the morning

2.

☐ a. a kitchen at 1:00 p.m.
☐ b. a living room at 9:00 p.m.

3.

☐ a. a bedroom in the summer
☐ b. a bedroom in the winter

B Read and listen. 33

This is the time and the place of the **setting**.

It's Sunday, and I'm at my grandparents' house. I help Grandma in the kitchen. Later, Grandpa and I work in the garden. My grandparents' house isn't big, but it's full of fun!

C Read **B** again. Why is the house special? Choose ✔ or ✘.

1. It has a garden.

2. It's full of fun.

3. It's big.

Read 🔊 34

What is the **setting**? Underline the time and place.

Small Houses, Big Heart

On April 25, 2015, there was an earthquake in Nepal. Mud and brick houses on the sides of mountains fell down. People went to live in camps. There weren't many bathrooms, and it was hard to wash up. Did they build big houses? No, they didn't. Did they get help? Yes, they did.

For example, people from Germany came and built earthbag houses. Earthbags are bags filled with dirt or sand. Each house was very small. It didn't have a dining room for eating, or a garage for cars, but the people were safe. Did people play games in their houses? Yes, they did. Did they sweep the floor? Yes, they did. The small earthbag houses were their homes.

Think!

- How can we help people who don't have homes?

Listen, point, and say.

bathroom

wash up

dining room

garage

play games

sweep the floor

Find the key words in the article. Then write them in your picture dictionary.

Understand

A Read *Small Houses, Big Heart* again. What kind of places did people live in before the earthquake? Choose **Yes** or **No**.

1. They lived in camps.   **Yes   No**

2. They lived in mud and brick houses.   **Yes   No**

3. They lived in big houses.   **Yes   No**

B Choose the correct answer.

1. Where did many people live after the earthquake in Nepal?

   ☐ a. in big houses   ☐ b. in camps

2. What was helpful after the earthquake?

   ☐ a. garages   ☐ b. small houses

3. Who helped in Nepal?

   ☐ a. people from Germany   ☐ b. people with cars

C Complete the sentences with key words. Then match.

1. It was hard to _____ after the earthquake.

2. The camps had few _____

3. The small houses did not have dining rooms or _____

4. Did people _____ to keep it clean?

a.

b.

c.

d.

_____   _____   _____   _____

D Read *Small Houses, Big Heart* again. What did people do after the earthquake? Complete the table. Work with a partner.

Did they … ?	Yes, they did.	No, they didn't.
1. get help	✔	
2. build big houses		
3. play games		
4. sweep the floor		

E Look at **D**. Write. Use *Did* in the question. Use *Yes, they did* or *No, they didn't* in the answer.

1.

2.

Did they get help?

Yes, they did.

_____

_____

3.

4.

_____

_____

_____

_____

MY READING GOALS

☐ I can read an article.

☐ I can understand the setting and identify how it affects people.

Reading Check

Remember!
Identify the **main characters**.
Who is the story about?
Understand the **setting**. How
does it affect people in the text?

A Read and listen. 36

A Fun House!

In the summer, the Smith family moves into a new house. They meet their new neighbors, the Fishers and the Kims. The Fishers say, "We saw your house. It's funny. There's one bedroom and four bathrooms." The friendly Smiths say, "It's a funny house for a funny family!" The Kims give them a big blanket. The Smiths move their beds into the bedroom, and each family member chooses a bathroom.

At 7:00 p.m., they make dinner in the kitchen and eat in the dining room. They play games in the living room. Then they get into their beds, share the big blanket, and go to sleep!

B Look for the main characters. Who are they? Choose ✔ or ✗.

1. The Smith family

2. The Fisher family

3. The Kim family

C Look for the setting. Where does this story take place? Choose ✔ or ✘.

1. at night at the Smiths' old house   ☑ ☒

2. in the summer at the Smiths' new house   ☑ ☒

3. at 7:00 p.m. at the Fishers' new house   ☑ ☒

D Choose the correct answer.

1. Who says the Smiths' house is funny?	**the Fishers**	**the Kims**
2. What do the Kims give the Smiths?	**dinner**	**a blanket**
3. Who is friendly?	**the Fishers**	**the Smiths**
4. How many bathrooms are there?	**four**	**one**
5. What do the Smiths do at 7:00 p.m.?	**make dinner**	**sleep**
6. Where do the Smiths play games?	**the dining room**	**the living room**

E Complete the sentences.

> play games   table   kitchen   bathrooms   beds
>
> bedroom   dining room   chair

1. There is one _____

2. There are four _____

3. At 7:00 p.m., the Smith family makes dinner in the

_____

4. They eat dinner in the _____

5. They _____ in the living room.

6. The Smiths put one blanket over all the _____

and go to sleep.

Get Ready to Write

WRITING GOAL: Write a Journal Entry

A *journal* is where you write what happened on a specific day. You can write about what you were doing and what you were thinking.

A **Read the journal entry. Underline the date.**

Writing Tip
Include the date at the top of your journal so you remember when you wrote it.

Thursday, May 23

Today, I went to my friend Tula's house.

First, we ate a snack in the dining room.

Tula's mom gave us watermelon, and it was yummy! Then we went to Tula's bedroom and watched a funny movie.

Then Tula's mom played some Greek music in the living room.

I even learned a Greek dance. I had a fun time.

B **Look at A. What did Callie do? Complete the diagram.**

1. Where did she go?

   She went to her friend Tula's house.

2. What did she eat?

   First, _____

   _____

Date: Thursday, May 23

3. What did she do?

   Then _____

   _____

4. What else did she do?

   Then _____

   _____

Write

C   Think about a time you visited a friend. Complete the diagram.

1. Where did you go?

I went to my friend

_____'s house.

Date:

_____
_____

2. What did you eat?

First, _____

_____

3. What did you do?

Then _____

_____

4. What else did you do?

Then _____

_____

D   Now write your own journal entry. Use words from **C**.
Choose new words, too. Then draw your friend's house.

Date: _____

Today, I went to my friend _____'s house.

First, _____

Then _____

Then _____

I had a fun time.

Now write a journal entry about a visit to
another place.

MY WRITING GOAL

☐   I can write a journal entry.

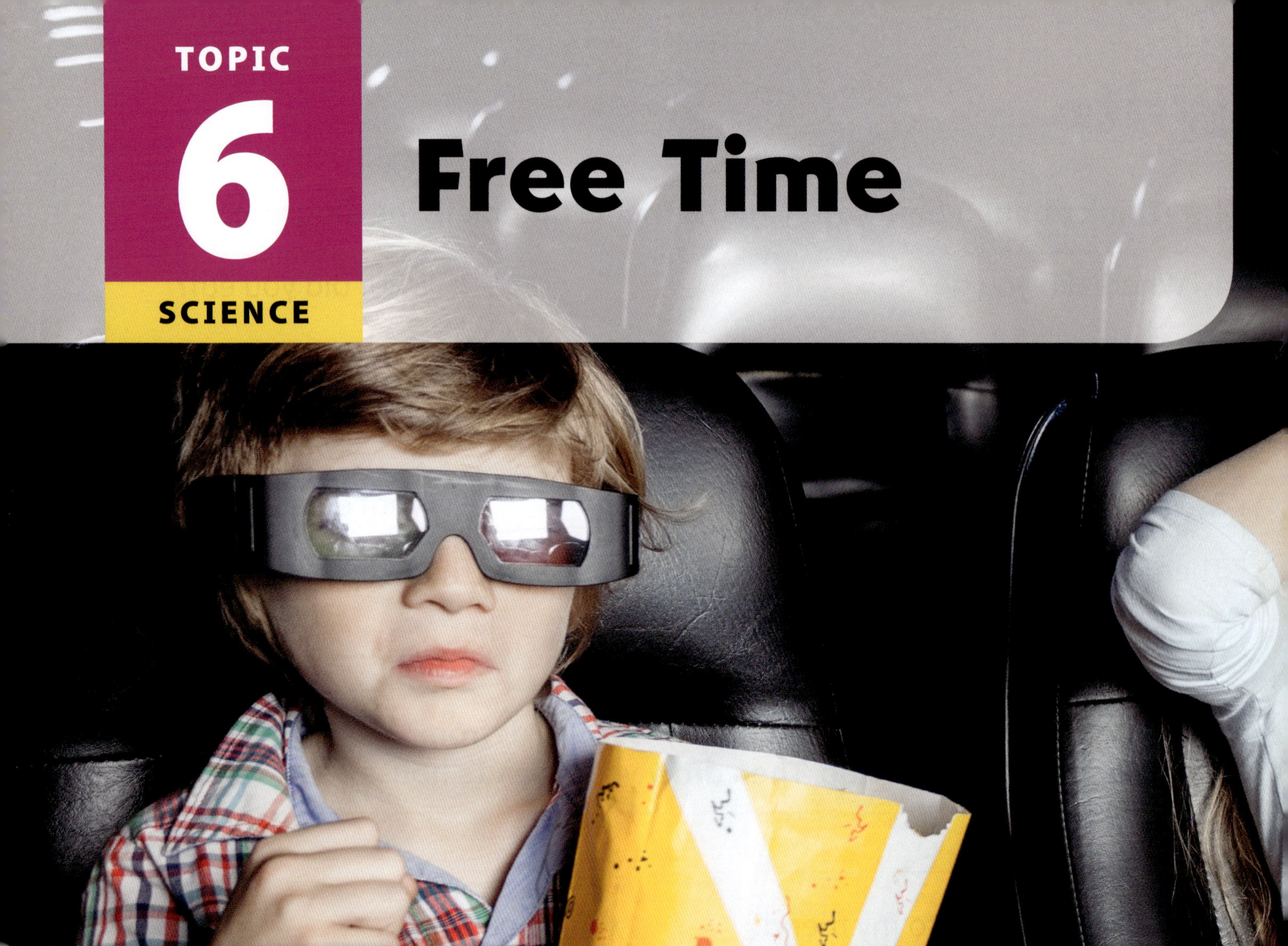

TOPIC

6 Free Time

SCIENCE

MY GOALS

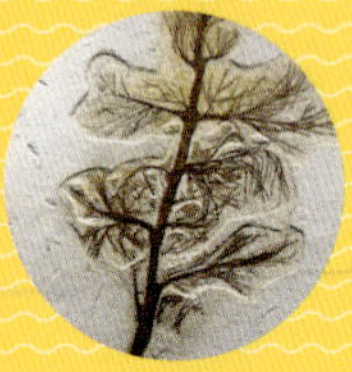

UNIT 11

- Read the article *Fossils Are Fun!*
- Understand the sequence of events

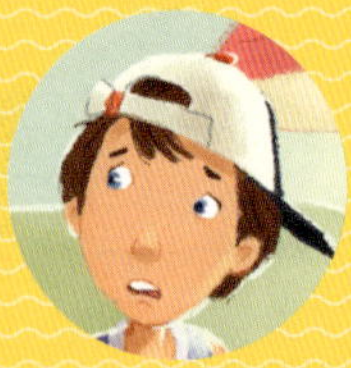

UNIT 12

- Read the story *The Broken TV*
- Find the beginning, middle, and end

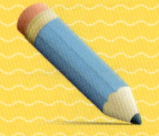

WRITE

- Write a story

A **Look at the picture. What do you see?**

1. Where are the people?
2. Why are they wearing glasses?

FUN FACT

The first movies were black and white, and didn't have sound. Movies with sound came 20 years later. Now we have 3-D movies, and we wear special glasses to watch them.

B Read the Fun Fact. Then answer the questions.

1. How are today's movies different from the first movies?

2. What kind of movies do you like?

Think, Pair, Share
What do you like to do in your free time? Why?

Get Ready to Read

READING GOAL: Understand the Sequence of Events

Events are things that happen in a text. The sequence of events is the order of things. Find words like *first*, *then*, and *finally* to help you understand the order things happen as you read.

A **Look at the pictures. What happens first? Order the actions.**

First, she walks to the beach.

Finally, she finishes the sandcastle.

Then she builds a sandcastle.

B **Read and listen.** 37

These words show the **order** of things in the text.

My dad likes to grow vegetables. First, he plants the seeds in his garden. He waters them every week in his free time. Then in a few weeks, the plants grow and make vegetables. Finally, my dad picks the vegetables and eats them as snacks!

C **Read B again. What is the order of events in the text? Choose the correct answer.**

   a. He eats the vegetables. He plants the seeds. He waters the seeds.

   b. He plants the seeds. He waters the seeds. He eats the vegetables.

   c. He picks the vegetables. He waters the seeds. He plants the seeds.

Read 38

What are the words that show the **sequence of events**? Underline them.

Fossils Are Fun!

Many people learn about fossils in their free time. It's a fun hobby. Fossils are very old things from plants and animals. You can see them in some rocks. There are even fossils of fish that used to swim in the ocean. How did these plants and animals become fossils? First, they died and dropped to the ground. Then dirt and other things covered them. Finally, after a long time, they changed into fossils.

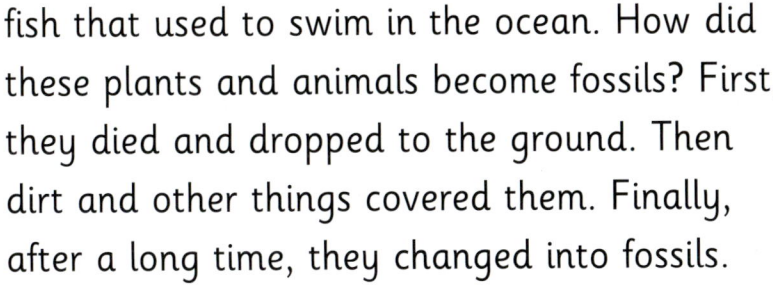

You may find a fossil when you play outside. You can go shopping for them at special stores, too. To learn more about fossils, read a book or use the computer.

Think!

Where can you look for fossils?

Key Words 39

Listen, point, and say.

learn about fossils

swim in the ocean

play outside

go shopping

read a book

use the computer

Find the key words in the article. Then write them in your picture dictionary.

Understand

A Read *Fossils Are Fun!* again. How did plants and animals change into fossils? Choose the correct answer.

☐ a. they died, things covered them, they changed into fossils

☐ b. things covered them, they died, they changed into fossils

B Choose the correct answer.

1. Fossils are parts of **plants and animals / computers and stores**.

2. People can **swim in the ocean / read a book** to learn about fossils.

3. People can find fossils **in plants / in rocks**.

C Complete the sentences.

| learn about fossils | go shopping | swim in the ocean |
| play outside | read a book | use the computer |

1.

People _____ in stores.

2.

Fish _____

3.

Look for fossils when you _____

4.

_____ to learn about fossils.

D Change the present tense verbs into the simple past tense. Complete the table.

Present Tense	Simple Past Tense
1. die	plants and animals ____died____
2. drop	they _____ to the ground
3. cover	dirt _____ them
4. change	they _____ into fossils

E Look at **D**. Use the simple past tense of the verb. Write.

1.

First, __plants and animals died.__
_____

2.

They _____
_____

3.

Then _____
_____

4.

Finally, _____
_____

MY READING GOALS

☐ I can read an article. ☐ I can find the order of things in a text and understand the sequence of events.

Get Ready to Read

READING GOAL: Find the Beginning, Middle, and End

A story has three parts. The *beginning* introduces the characters and the setting. The *middle* introduces the problem and shows what happens. The *end* has the solution to the problem.

A Look at the pictures. What part of the story is each picture? Choose the correct answer.

1.

☐ a. beginning
☐ b. middle

2.

☐ a. beginning
☐ b. middle

3.

☐ a. middle
☐ b. end

B Read and listen. 40

A story has a **beginning**, **middle**, and **end**.

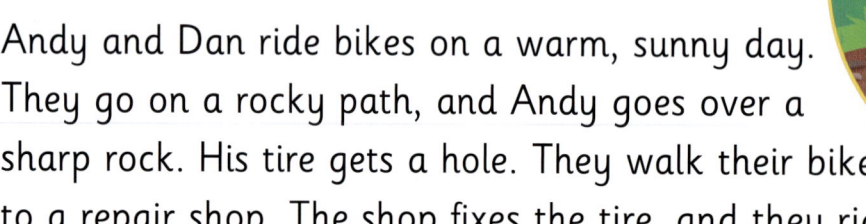

Andy and Dan ride bikes on a warm, sunny day. They go on a rocky path, and Andy goes over a sharp rock. His tire gets a hole. They walk their bikes to a repair shop. The shop fixes the tire, and they ride home.

C Read **B** again. What is the problem in the middle of the story? Choose ✔ or ✘.

1. Andy rides his bike with Dan.

2. Andy's tire gets a hole.

3. Andy rides his bike home.   ✔

Read 41

Can you find the **three parts** of the story? Write **B** by the beginning, **M** by the middle, and **E** by the end.

The Broken TV

Every day, Evan stays home and watches TV in his living room. He loves action shows. One day, the TV doesn't work, and Evan says, "We need a new TV!" His mom says, "Dad can fix it. Do other things in your free time." Dad looks at the TV, and he says, "Sorry, it's really broken." Evan sits around for a few days. Then he gets busy! He goes mountain biking on Monday. He practices piano on Tuesday. He plays video games on Wednesday. He goes skateboarding on Thursday. He sleeps in a tent on Friday. Finally, they buy a new TV, and it's better than the old one!

Think!

How much TV do you watch every day in your free time?

Key Words 42

Listen, point, and say.

stay home

go mountain biking

practice piano

play video games

go skateboarding

sleep in a tent

Find the key words in the story. Then write them in your picture dictionary.

Understand

Remember!
Find the **beginning**, the **middle**, and the **end**. The story begins with characters and setting. The middle has a problem. The end has a solution.

A Read *The Broken TV* again. What happens in the beginning, the middle, and the end? Choose **Yes** or **No**.

1. In the beginning, Evan doesn't watch TV.   **Yes**   **No**

2. In the middle, the TV breaks.   **Yes**   **No**

3. In the end, they get a new TV.   **Yes**   **No**

B Choose the correct answer.

1. Where does Evan watch TV?

☐ a. in the living room   ☐ b. in a tent

2. What does Evan do on Thursday?

☐ a. He plays video games.   ☐ b. He goes skateboarding.

3. Does Evan like the new TV?

☐ a. Yes, he does.   ☐ b. No, he doesn't.

C Complete the sentences with key words. Then match.

1. On Friday, Evan _____

2. Evan _____ on Monday.

3. Evan likes to _____ and watch TV.

4. Evan _____ on Thursday.

a.

b.

c.

d.

_____   _____   _____   _____

D Read *The Broken TV* again. What does Evan do on each day? Complete the diagram. Work with a partner.

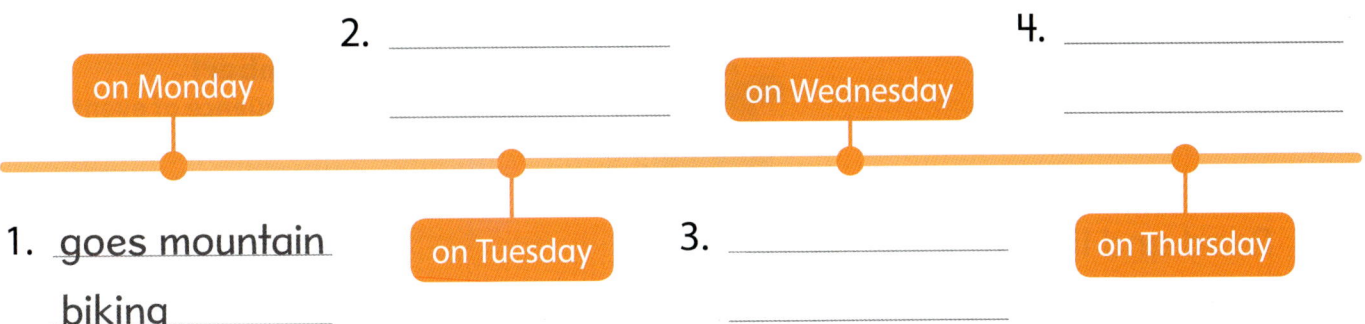

2. _____
_____

on Monday

on Wednesday

4. _____
_____

1. goes mountain biking

on Tuesday

3. _____

on Thursday

E Look at **D**. Write. Use *on* and the day of the week.

1.

He goes mountain biking
on Monday.

2.

_____
_____

3.

_____
_____

4.

_____
_____

MY READING GOALS

☐ I can read a story.

☐ I can find the beginning, middle, and end of a story.

Reading Check

A Read and listen.  43

Always Bring Bikes!

The Miller family was ready for their summer vacation. The car was packed and ready to go.

First, Mr. Miller drove, but the car started making funny noises. After a while, Mrs. Miller drove, but it made the same noises. The family worried about the car getting to the beach. Then the car stopped working. Mr. Miller said, "It's a good thing we packed our bikes."

The family rode their bikes to a nearby car repair shop, and found a nice woman to fix their car. Finally, it was time to swim in the ocean and play outside. The Miller family was happy.

B Look for the sequence of events. What happens first? Choose ✔ or ✘.

1. Mr. Miller drove the car.

2. The family used their bikes.   ✔   ✘

3. The car stopped working.

C Look for the beginning, middle, and end. What happens in each part of the story? Choose ✔ or ✘.

1. In the beginning, they used their bikes. ✔ ✘

2. In the middle, the car stopped working. ✔ ✘

3. In the end, Mr. Miller drove. ✔ ✘

D Choose the correct answer.

1. When does this story take place?

  ☐ a. spring vacation   ☐ b. summer vacation

2. Mr. Miller says it's a good thing the family _____

  ☐ a. brought their bikes.   ☐ b. swam in the ocean.

3. The sisters were _____ at the end.

  ☐ a. worried   ☐ b. happy

E Unscramble and match.

1. k a t e s a n p a

   _____   •   • a. Sue _____ so her fingers are strong.

2. a p y l t u o s d i e

   _____   •   • b. They _____ for fresh fruit every day.

3. c c t i r p a e s o p a i n

   _____   •   • c. Kim likes to _____ more than inside.

4. e d a r a o b k o

   _____   •   • d. My brother _____ and wakes up happy.

5. y a s t m e h o

   _____   •   • e. Max's favorite place to _____ is in a library.

6. o g p s p h n i o g

   _____   •   • f. I don't want to go out. Let's _____ instead.

Get Ready to Write

WRITING GOAL: Write a Story
A story has a beginning, middle, and end. Make sure to write all the parts in your story so readers have a complete story.

A Read the story. Underline the setting and the description.

> **Writing Tip**
> Describe the setting in the story to paint a picture in the reader's mind.

A Shell for Sasha

Bruno walks on the beautiful, white beach. He's looking for shells. It's early in the afternoon, and the sun is high in the sky. Bruno wants to find a special shell for his friend Sasha. He walks for an hour and doesn't see any shells.

Then a big wave crashes on the beach. After the water from the wave goes back into the ocean, Bruno sees a beautiful, pink shell in the sand. It's perfect for Sasha.

B Look at **A**. What happens in each part of the story? Complete the timeline.

Beginning	Middle	End
1. Bruno walks on the beach. He's looking for shells.	2. _____	3. _____

Write

C Think about a story. Describe two things that happen in each part of the story. Complete the timeline.

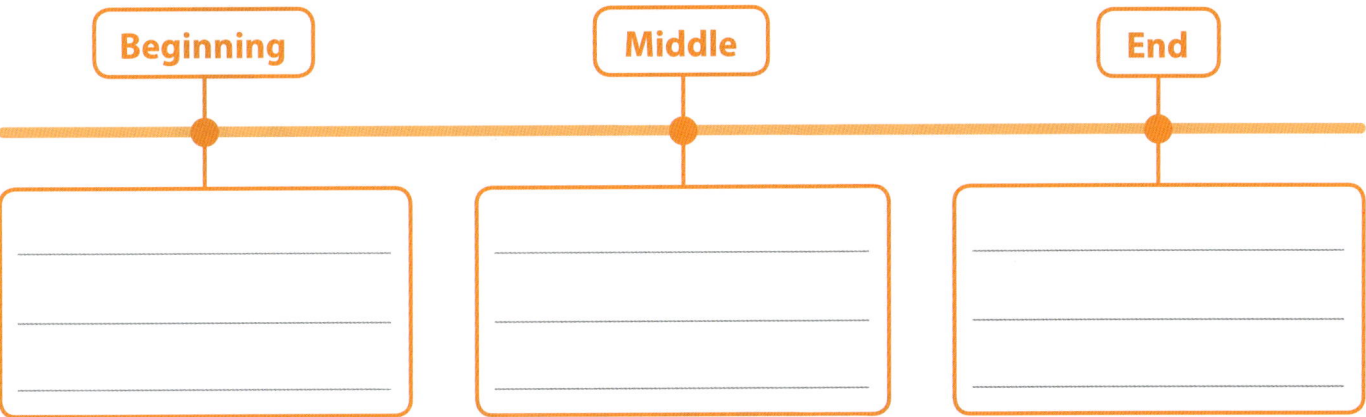

| Beginning | Middle | End |

D Now write the story. Use your words from **C**. Choose new words, too. Then draw a main character.

(The Beginning: Character + Setting)

_____

(The Middle: Problem)

_____

_____

(The End: Solution)

_____

 Now write another story with a beginning, middle, and end.

MY WRITING GOAL

☐ I can write a story.

Reading with Writing 3

Workbook

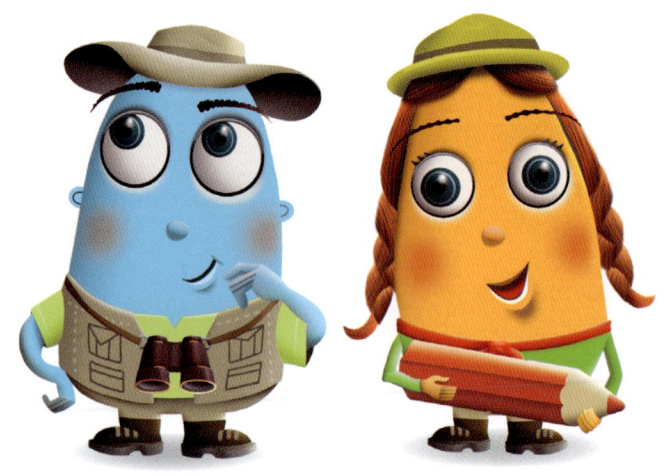

Yoko Mia Hirano

OXFORD
UNIVERSITY PRESS

Read

READING GOAL:
Skim for Gist

A Skim the article. What is it about?

From Bottles to Buildings

Greenhouses are buildings that help plants grow in cold weather. The sun keeps plants warm in a greenhouse. You can make one with water bottles. This is a fun project! First, keep your water bottles so you can use them for this project. When you have enough water bottles, draw a plan. This drawing is your guide. Now you can build your greenhouse. Glue together the water bottles into walls and a roof. Don't forget to make a door! Finally, you can use your paintbrushes and paint to decorate.

B Read the article. Then choose the correct answer.

1. What is the gist of the article?
   - ☐ a. Water bottles are fun.
   - ☐ b. Keep water bottles.
   - ☑ c. Use water bottles to make a greenhouse.

2. What are greenhouses for?
   - ☐ a. growing plants
   - ☐ b. water bottles
   - ☐ c. painting houses

3. What can you use as a plan?
   - ☐ a. a roof
   - ☐ b. glue
   - ☐ c. a drawing

4. What do you glue together for walls?
   - ☐ a. plants
   - ☐ b. water bottles
   - ☐ c. doors

C Trace the words. Then choose the correct picture for each word.

1. _____ smock _____

☐ a.   ☑ b.

2. _____ paintbrush _____

☐ a.   ☐ b.

3. _____ paint _____

☐ a.   ☐ b.

4. _____ door _____

☐ a.   ☐ b.

D Complete the sentences.

| door | paint | glue | paintbrushes | smocks |
| table | paper clips | water bottles |

1. Mark opens the _____ so Sara can come in the house.

2. Sara and Mark wear _____

3. They have buckets of red and yellow _____

4. They use big _____ to paint the wall.

5. They use old _____ to hold the paintbrushes.

6. They set up everything on the _____

Read

READING GOAL:
Scan for Details

Remember!
Scan for **details** to find more information. Read the text quickly and look for color words or numbers.

A Read the e-mail. Think about details as you read.

TO: Meri   **FROM:** Amy

SUBJECT: A Cool Project

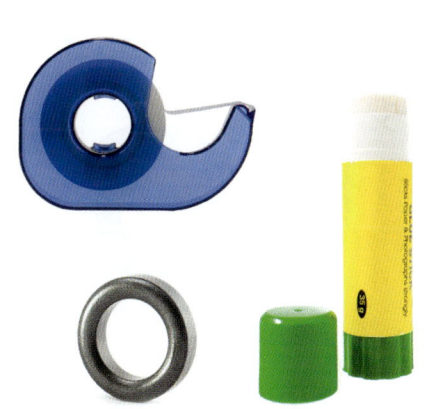

Do you have any magazines? I have some, but I need more. I'm looking for fun ones. I'm doing a cool project. I'm cutting out ten pictures. I'm using a glue stick to stick pictures to magnets. They're coming out great.

Do you want to come over today? I can show you five magnets. I'm making one for you. That makes six magnets! We can also paint old water bottles. I use them as pencil and marker holders. I have ten different paint colors and seven water bottles. We can paint each bottle a different color!

Your friend,

Amy

Animal World

Horses!

B Read again. Then choose the correct answer.

1. Amy has ten paint colors. This is a detail.   **Yes**   **No**
2. Amy is looking for fun magazines.   **Yes**   **No**
3. Amy doesn't want Meri to come over.   **Yes**   **No**
4. Amy is making a magnet for Meri.   **Yes**   **No**
5. Amy asks Meri for glue sticks.   **Yes**   **No**
6. Amy has ten water bottles.   **Yes**   **No**

C Complete the sentences.

computer   magazine   tape   glue stick   magnets   string

1.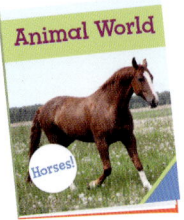

   Cary is reading a _____

2.

   Jake turns on the _____

3.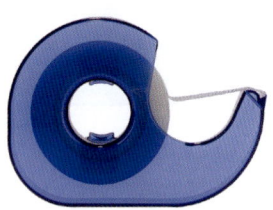

   Mehmet has some _____

4.

   Becky ties the _____

D Complete the paragraph.

Here's a great project to do at home. Get some (1) _magnets_

to make a magnet weight. It can hold down papers. First, use

(2) _t_____ to hold the magnets together. You can use string

to tie the magnets together, too. Then cut out fun pictures from

(3) _m_____. Use a (4) _g_____ to stick the pictures on

the magnet weight.

Write

Remember!
Use details to give more
information in your description.

Underline the details.

We're doing a science project at school. We're planting nine
brown seeds. Then we're watching them for two weeks.

Read

READING GOAL:
Find Facts

A Read the article. Think about the facts as you read.

Making Clothes Better

We make more clothes than we need. We make dresses, socks, and shoes in different sizes and colors. It's fun to have lots of clothes to choose from, but some of the things we make these clothes from can be bad for nature.

We are starting to make clothes like jackets and skirts in better ways. Some people make clothes from old water bottles. Others use old clothes to make new clothes. People also make clothes from trees. It's important to learn new ways to make clothes. It's good to know our new clothes don't hurt nature.

B Read again. Then choose the correct answer.

1. What fact is in *Making Clothes Better*?

    ☐ a. It's fun to choose clothes.   ☐ b. Nature is bad for clothes.

    ☐ c. People make clothes in different sizes and colors.

2. What is the text mainly about?

    ☐ a. buying clothes   ☐ b. making clothes   ☐ c. wearing clothes

3. What can be bad for nature?

    ☐ a. clothes in different sizes   ☐ b. shirts and pants

    ☐ c. some of the things we make clothes from

4. What is a better way to make clothes?

    ☐ a. having lots of choices   ☐ b. making different sizes

    ☐ c. using old clothes to make new ones

C Trace the words. Then choose the correct picture for each word.

1. _____gloves_____

☐ a. ☐ b.

2. _____hat_____

☐ a. ☐ b.

3. _____jacket_____

☐ a. ☐ b.

4. _____boots_____

☐ a. ☐ b.

D Complete the sentences.

| socks | boots | gloves | smocks | jacket | shirt | hat | backpack |

1. It's very cold outside, so Kim is wearing a warm _____ under her jacket.

2. Jody has soft _____ on her feet.

3. Yusef wears a big, puffy, black _____ , and it covers his shirt and sweater.

4. Adam's _____ is small for his head.

5. Ela wears red _____ on her hands.

6. Tony puts heavy, blue _____ on his feet and walks to school in the snow.

Read

READING GOAL:
Find Opinions

Remember!
Opinions are what a person thinks about things.

A Read the story. Think about the opinions as you read.

Fancy Snow Boots

Alan lives in warm, sunny Sydney, Australia, but he loves boots and he wears them every day.

One day, he sees fancy snow boots on TV. He thinks, "I have so many boots, but I think those boots are really nice!" That night, he can't sleep, because he feels excited.

In the morning, he puts on his favorite green shirt and blue jeans. He calls his best friend and says, "Joanne, I want fancy snow boots. Can you help me find them?" Joanne says, "Alan, you don't need fancy snow boots! It never snows here!" Alan says, "You're right. Thanks, Joanne!"

B Read again. Then choose the correct answer.

1. Alan lives in a warm place. This is an opinion. **Yes** **No**
2. Does Alan see snow boots in a magazine? **Yes** **No**
3. Does Alan have many boots? **Yes** **No**
4. Does Alan sleep that night? **Yes** **No**
5. Does Joanne help Alan find the boots? **Yes** **No**
6. Does it snow in Sydney, Australia? **Yes** **No**

C Complete the sentences.

| skirt | pants | dress | shoes | sweater | jeans |

1.

Those are nice _____

2.

Ed wears _____

3.

_____ are on sale today!

4.

Sarah likes her new _____

D Complete the sentences.

1. I put socks and s_____ on my feet.

2. She likes her red j_____ because it's warm.

3. His p_____ are short.

4. It's cold, so I'm wearing this s_____

Write

Underline the opinion.

Come to the fair. I think it's fun because there are lots of games.

Remember!
Use *I think* and *I feel* to write opinions, and *because* to give reasons.

Read

READING GOAL:
Find the Problem and Solution

A Read the story. Think about the problem and solution.

Lost in London

Mom runs ahead of us, so I shout, "Where are you going?" She shouts back, "A bakery. It's about to close, Nina. Please get your brother!"

I grab my backpack and say, "Hurry, Doug! Mom is ahead of us." He's taking photos and says, "This park is more interesting than bakeries or stores." My voice gets louder. "It's going to get dark, and we're lost!" Doug opens his London map. "Where did she go?" he asks. "A bakery. I don't know its name. I'm calling her right now to get directions," I say.

B Read again. Then choose the correct answer.

1. What is the problem?

☐ a. It's dark. ☐ b. They're lost. ☐ c. They can't find the park.

2. Nina and Doug solve the problem by …

☐ a. calling mom. ☐ b. using a map. ☐ c. shouting for help.

3. Where are Nina and Doug?

☐ a. in a bakery ☐ b. in a store ☐ c. in a park

4. What is Doug doing?

☐ a. calling his mom ☐ b. taking photos ☐ c. running ahead

C Trace the words. Then choose the correct picture for each word.

1. _____ bakery _____

☐ a. ☐ b.

2. _____ park _____

☐ a. ☐ b.

3. _____ bus station _____

☐ a. ☐ b.

4. _____ office _____

☐ a. ☐ b.

D Complete the sentences.

park	bakery	school	office	store
	bus station	classroom	library	

1. Can we go out to play at the _____

2. Sam is hungry. Let's get some cookies from the _____

3. The bus is at the _____

4. Dad has meetings in his _____

5. Let's get books at the _____

6. A new toy _____ is coming.

Read

READING GOAL:
Classify

Remember!
Classifying is putting things in a group because they are similar in some way.

A Read. How are some stores similar? Classify them.

Shop Until You Drop!

The Grove is a cool shopping mall in Los Angeles, California. It's very big, so make a plan before you go.

What do you want to buy? You can shop at clothing stores or at a toy store. You can see different kinds of computers in a computer store. You can look at books and magazines at a bookstore.

Are you hungry? You can eat a meal at a restaurant, or a snack at a snack shop.

Finally, do you want to see a movie? The movie theater can show ten movies at one time!

B Read again. Then choose the correct answer.

1. Do bookstores, toy stores, and computer stores sell things?   **Yes**   **No**

2. Do restaurants and snack shops sell food?   **Yes**   **No**

3. Is there a gym at The Grove?   **Yes**   **No**

4. Are there places to eat a meal at The Grove?   **Yes**   **No**

5. Is there a train station at The Grove?   **Yes**   **No**

6. Can the movie theater show eleven movies?   **Yes**   **No**

C Complete the sentences.

> gym   train station   movie theater   shopping mall
>
> factory   shoe repair shop

1.

The _____ has yummy popcorn!

2.

Let's exercise at the _____

3.

The _____ has many stores.

4.

The _____ is near the park.

D Complete the sentences.

1. People like buying things at the _s_____

2. A _s_____ can fix boots, too.

3. Tara isn't going to work in a _f_____

4. What movies are playing at the _m_____ tonight?

Write

Underline the sequence words.

> **Remember!**
> A process paragraph uses sequence words *first*, *then*, *next*, and *finally*.

Are you going to a city? First, buy good shoes for walking. Then get a map. Next, plan places to visit. Finally, bring a camera!

Read

READING GOAL:
Make Notes

Remember!
Make **notes** to help you
remember the important
information in a text.

A Read the article. Make notes about important things in the text.

Larry the Lifeguard

Meet Larry! He's a lifeguard at the city beach. Larry's job is hard, but he really likes it. He sits in a tall chair and watches kids and adults as they swim or play in the water. He makes sure they stay safe and have fun at the same time. He also looks at the weather. When it gets too windy or stormy, he shouts at people to get out of the water.

Larry doesn't want to be a lifeguard forever. Someday he wants to be a builder or an actor. But for now, Larry is happy. He gets to sit in the sun and help people.

My notes:

B Read again. Then choose the correct answer. You can use your notes.

1. What is a note about this text?
   - [ ] a. Larry likes his job.
   - [ ] b. The beach is windy.
   - [ ] c. Larry isn't happy.

2. What do lifeguards do?
   - [ ] a. play in water
   - [ ] b. yell at people
   - [ ] c. keep people safe

3. Lifeguards tell people to get out of the water because …
   - [ ] a. it's sunny.
   - [ ] b. it's stormy.
   - [ ] c. it's fun.

4. Larry like his job because …
   - [ ] a. he is safe.
   - [ ] b. he helps people.
   - [ ] c. it's windy.

C Trace the words. Then choose the correct picture for each word.

1. _baseball player_

☐ a. ☐ b.

2. _actor_

☐ a. ☐ b.

3. _photographer_

☐ a. ☐ b.

4. _lifeguard_

☐ a. ☐ b.

D Complete the sentences.

actor	baseball player	bus driver	photographer	builder
	lifeguard	mother	veterinarian	

1. The _____ runs quickly around the field.

2. The _____ is in TV shows and movies.

3. Roy is bringing his dog to the _____

4. The _____ takes good pictures.

5. The _____ works at a pool.

6. My sister is a _____. She's working on a new house.

Read

READING GOAL:
Summarize

Remember!
Summarize to tell what a story is about in one or two sentences.

A Read the story. Summarize what the story is about.

Sunday Lunch

Barry has a big family. He has four sisters and brothers. They all have jobs.

His older sister is a pilot. His younger sister is an artist. His older brother is a baker. His younger brother is a farmer.

They all meet once a week on Sunday for lunch. They have a lot of fun.

His younger brother brings corn and eggs from the farm. His younger sister paints their pictures. His older brother bakes cookies, and his older sister gives everybody a ride in her plane.

Barry loves his big family, and Sunday is his favorite day of the week!

B Read again. Then choose the correct answer.

1. Barry has sisters. This is a good summary.   **Yes**   **No**
2. Does Barry have two brothers?   **Yes**   **No**
3. Do they all meet every Saturday?   **Yes**   **No**
4. Does one brother bring animals?   **Yes**   **No**
5. Do they share things from work?   **Yes**   **No**
6. Does Barry's older brother bake cookies?   **Yes**   **No**

C Complete the sentences.

| salesclerk | artist | pilot | baker | teacher | farmer |

1.

A _____ works in a store.

2.

This _____ paints pictures.

3.

The _____ grows food.

4.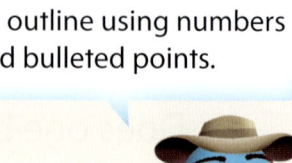

A _____ makes bread.

D Complete the sentences.

1. The f_____ gives his animals food.

2. The p_____ flies planes.

3. Tim is looking for the s_____ in the store.

4. The t_____ reads a book to the class.

Write

Remember!
Write an outline using numbers and bulleted points.

Underline the numbers. Circle the bulleted points.

1. Barry has two sisters.
   - older sister – pilot
   - younger sister – artist

2. Barry has two brothers.
   - older brother – baker
   - younger brother – farmer

Read

READING GOAL: Identify the Main and Minor Characters

A Read the story. Can you find the main character? Underline him or her.

A Path in the Snow

Carl looked out the window at the snow. His friend Silvia waved for him to come out, but he pointed at his broken leg. She said, "Sorry! I forgot." He was bored in his small house. He was always in the living room, the kitchen, or his bedroom. He read a book and watched TV. Later, his friends came to the front door. Silvia and Tomas pointed to a path in the snow. They helped Carl into his wheelchair and went outside. He loved the sun, the blue sky, and the cold air. Most of all, he loved his friends.

B Read again. Then choose the correct answer.

1. How do the minor characters help the main character in the story?
   - [ ] a. They read a book to him.
   - [ ] b. They wave to him.
   - [ ] c. They take him outside.

2. What is the weather like outside?
   - [ ] a. rainy
   - [ ] b. windy
   - [ ] c. sunny

3. Carl is in …
   - [ ] a. his friend's house.
   - [ ] b. a small house.
   - [ ] c. a big house.

4. Carl's broken leg …
   - [ ] a. keeps him inside.
   - [ ] b. hurts.
   - [ ] c. makes him happy.

C Trace the words. Then choose the correct picture for each word.

1. _living room_

☐ a. ☐ b.

2. _bedroom_

☐ a. ☐ b.

3. _lamp_

☐ a. ☐ b.

4. _bed_

☐ a. ☐ b.

D Complete the sentences.

bed	living room	couch	desk	bedroom
lamp	kitchen	wastebasket		

1. The bed is in the _____

2. Turn on the _____ , please. It's dark in here.

3. Let's sit on the _____ in the living room.

4. Mom is cooking in the _____

5. Tom is sitting on the couch in the _____

6. Carol is sleeping in her _____ , under a warm blanket.

Read

READING GOAL:
Understand the Setting

Remember!
Understand the **setting** so you know the time and place of the text as you read.

A Read the article. What is the setting? Underline it.

Sweden's Small Houses

A great place to visit in the summer is Gothenburg, Sweden. It's a big city near the water. It has lots of exciting things, like museums, parks, and stores.

It also has some groups of very small, red houses. People take long summer vacations in these little houses. They enjoy the warm weather and long, sunny days.

Each small house has a kitchen to cook in, a bathroom to wash up in, and a bedroom to sleep in. They don't have dining rooms or garages. They also have small gardens, and people grow food.

These little houses are easy to get to and fun to live in!

Do you have a plan for the summer? A small house in Gothenburg, Sweden, is a great vacation idea!

B Read again. Then choose the correct answer.

1. Is the setting in Gothenburg, Sweden, in the winter? **Yes** **No**
2. Is the article about growing food in Sweden? **Yes** **No**
3. Do these small houses have dining rooms? **Yes** **No**
4. Do these small houses have kitchens? **Yes** **No**
5. Can people take vacations in these small houses? **Yes** **No**
6. Are these small houses hard to get to? **Yes** **No**

dining room   wash up   bathroom   play games

garage   sweep the floor

1.

Dan can _____ today.

2.

Please _____ in the bathroom.

3.

The kids _____ all day.

4.

We eat in the _____

D **Complete the sentences.**

1. Kira washes her face in the b_____

2. There are cars in the g_____

3. Robin can s_____ with a broom later.

4. It is raining. Amir doesn't want to p_____ now.

Write

Underline the date.

April 22

Today is Earth Day. We plant trees and recycle cans today.

> **Remember!**
> Include the date at the top of your journal so you remember when you wrote it.

Read

READING GOAL: Understand the Sequence of Events

> **Remember!**
> Find the **sequence of events** to understand the order of things. *First*, *then*, and *finally* help you find the order.

A Read. Can you find the order of things?

Learning to Swim

Learning to swim takes time and practice. Different people learn in different ways. Can people learn to swim by reading a book? Maybe some people can, but most people need swimming lessons. First, most people take lessons and learn swimming skills from a teacher. Then they have some skills that they can practice in their free time. Next, some people need more lessons. Other people are fine on their own. Finally, when people can swim on their own, they can swim in the ocean, swim in the lake, or swim in a pool. There are so many places you can go!

B Read again. Then choose the correct answer.

1. What do you do first when you learn how to swim?
   ☐ a. take lessons   ☐ b. read a book   ☐ c. swim in the ocean

2. What is good to practice in your free time?
   ☐ a. taking lessons   ☐ b. reading a book   ☐ c. swimming skills

3. After getting swimming lessons, what do some people need?
   ☐ a. more lessons   ☐ b. a book   ☐ c. free time

4. What can you do in the ocean, the lake, and a pool?
   ☐ a. go places   ☐ b. swim on your own   ☐ c. read a book

C Trace the words. Then choose the correct picture for each word.

1. learn about fossils

☐ a.   ☐ b.

2. use the computer

☐ a.   ☐ b.

3. play outside

☐ a.   ☐ b.

4. read a book

☐ a.   ☐ b.

D Complete the sentences.

reads a book	learn about fossils	sweep the floor	play outside
wash up	play video games	use the computer	go shopping

1. My sister is going to _____ at the new clothing store.

2. It's raining, so we can't _____ today.

3. Do you _____ alone, or do you play them with friends?

4. We're going to _____ in our science class.

5. Jim wants to _____ to write, but it's broken.

6. Wendy _____ about animals to her little brother.

Read

READING GOAL: Find the Beginning, Middle, and End

Remember!
Find the three story parts. The **beginning** introduces characters and setting. The **middle** introduces the problem, and the **end** has the solution.

A Read the story. Can you find the three parts?

A Bear Scare!

The day of the camping trip is sunny and cold. Mike and Keri jump out of the camp leader's car. Mike is happy to be outside and look for frogs. Keri doesn't like the outdoors. She likes to practice piano or play video games inside.

First, they hike and make their tents. Then they hear a strange sound, and a bear shows up! The kids are scared. The camp leader puts his finger to his lips and says, "Shh." He throws a bag of food near the bear. Finally, it takes the bag and runs off.

Mike starts laughing. "What's so funny?" asks Keri. "I wanted to eat that food. I'm glad I didn't!" said Mike.

B Read again. Then choose the correct answer.

1. Does the bear come in the middle of the story?   **Yes**   **No**
2. Does Mike like the outdoors?   **Yes**   **No**
3. Does Keri like the outdoors?   **Yes**   **No**
4. Do they make their tents?   **Yes**   **No**
5. Does the bear run after them?   **Yes**   **No**
6. Does the bear take a bag of food?   **Yes**   **No**

C Complete the sentences.

practice piano   sleep in a tent   go mountain biking

go skateboarding   plays video games   stay home

1.

Scott likes to _____

2.

_____ more, and you get

better at playing it.

3.

Tina _____ in her

free time.

4.

Let's _____ at the park.

D Complete the sentences.

1. Ellen is going to s_____ at night.

2. Let's s_____ tonight. I'm tired.

3. Wear your bathing suit so we can s_____

4. Gus loves music, so he p_____ every day.

Write

Underline the setting.

Remember!
Describe the setting in the story to paint a picture in the reader's mind.

Jeff sits in his warm kitchen in the afternoon. The sun is
coming in the big windows, and the white walls look yellow.

Picture Dictionary

Write the key words.

Unit 1

_____

_____

_____

_____

_____

_____

Unit 2

_____

_____

_____

_____

_____

_____

Unit 3

_____

_____

_____

_____

_____

_____

Unit 4

_____

_____

_____

_____

_____

_____

Picture Dictionary

Unit 5

_____

_____

_____

_____

_____

_____

Unit 6

_____

_____

_____

_____

_____

_____

Unit 7

_____

_____

_____

_____

_____

_____

Unit 8

_____

_____

_____

_____

_____

_____

Unit 9

_____

_____

_____

_____

_____

_____

Unit 10

_____

_____

_____

_____

_____

_____

Unit 11

_____

_____

_____

_____

_____

_____

Unit 12

_____

_____

_____

_____

_____

_____

Syllabus

Topic	Unit	Reading Goal	Key Words	Writing Goal
TOPIC 1 Cool Projects	Unit 1	Skim for Gist	smock, paint, paintbrush, table, door, water bottle	Write a Description
	Unit 2	Scan for Details	computer, magnet, string, glue stick, magazine, tape	Focus: Details
TOPIC 2 Clothes for Everyone!	Unit 3	Find Facts	hat, gloves, socks, boots, shirt, jacket	Write a Persuasive Text
	Unit 4	Find Opinions	dress, jeans, shoes, skirt, sweater, pants	Focus: Opinions and Reasons
TOPIC 3 Lost in the Big City!	Unit 5	Find the Problem and Solution	office, library, bakery, bus station, park, store	Write a Process Paragraph
	Unit 6	Classify	movie theater, gym, train station, shopping mall, factory, shoe repair shop	Focus: Sequence Words
TOPIC 4 What's Your Job?	Unit 7	Make Notes	lifeguard, photographer, veterinarian, actor, baseball player, builder	Write an Outline
	Unit 8	Summarize	artist, farmer, baker, salesclerk, teacher, pilot	Focus: Main Ideas and Details
TOPIC 5 Small Houses	Unit 9	Identify the Main and Minor Characters	couch, living room, kitchen, lamp, bedroom, bed	Write a Journal Entry
	Unit 10	Understand the Setting	bathroom, wash up, dining room, garage, play games, sweep the floor	Focus: Dates
TOPIC 6 Free Time	Unit 11	Understand the Sequence of Events	learn about fossils, swim in the ocean, play outside, go shopping, read a book, use the computer	Write a Story
	Unit 12	Find the Beginning, Middle, and End	stay home, go mountain biking, practice piano, play video games, go skateboarding, sleep in a tent	Focus: Setting